BLUE D

The transformation of Chelsea under Hoddle, Gullit and Vialli.

Chris Wright

Blue Days
Copyright Chris Wright 2020
ISBN: 979-8564762144
THE MORAL RIGHT OF THE AUTHOR HAS BEEN ASSERTED
Apart from any fair dealing for the purposes of research or private study, or criticism or review, as permitted under the Copyright, Designs and Patents Act 1988, this publication may only be reproduced, stored or transmitted, in any means, with the prior permission in writing of GATE 17, or in the case of reprographic reproduction in accordance with the terms of licenses issued by the Copyright Licensing Agency. Enquiries concerning reproduction outside those terms should be sent to the publishers.

Twitter: @chriswrightzz
Front cover artwork: www.stephssketches.co.uk
Rear cover photo: Chris Wright
www.gate17.co.uk

CONTENTS

ACKNOWLEDGEMENTS 1
INTRODUCTION 4
1993 - 1994 6
1994 - 1995 24
1995 - 1996 36
1996 - 1997 50
1997 - 1998 69
1998 - 1999 89
1999 - 2000 108
2000 - 2001 123
CONCLUSION 127

ACKNOWLEDGEMENTS

A big thank you to Mark Worrall and Tim Rolls for making this book possible.

BLUE DAYS

This book is dedicated to my wonderful wife Jo and my two beautiful children Jack and Emily.

INTRODUCTION

Being born into a football supporting family in the early 1980's I was always going to follow in my dad's footsteps of supporting Chelsea as did my two brothers. Although my mum Sandra has no interest in football she has continued to support me in anything I've chosen to do and has always been there when I've needed her most. With my Nana living in Fulham at the time when I was growing up we would often coincide a match with seeing her. From my very first visit to Stamford Bridge in the 1989/90 season I never looked back and was always looking forward to my next match. My earliest memories were standing in The Shed with my dad and brothers and we'd bring a little foot stool in with us so I could see. The guys on the turnstiles would often let us in for free as they did for many children in those days. Win, lose or draw it didn't really bother me. The atmosphere in The Shed, the programme, the smell of hotdogs and onions and don't get me wrong, if Kerry Dixon popped up with a winner it was extra special.

In 1993 my dad surprised me by making me the Chelsea mascot for a game. At the age of ten it was a truly magical experience meeting my heroes, leading the team out and scoring past Stamford the lion in front of The Shed. My first trip to Wembley was the 1994 F.A Cup semi-final, a very memorable day but heart-breaking to lose the final the way we did. However I'm sure many will agree it made the 1997 victory that little bit more special.

What Roman Abramovich has achieved with the club since taking over in 2003 is quite remarkable and as fans our dreams really have come true and I'll be forever grateful for that.

Many rival fans taunt Chelsea saying the club was formed in 2003 and we don't have any history before that. This book will revisit and tell the story of when things really changed at Chelsea which was in the

BLUE DAYS

summer of 1993 with the arrival of Glenn Hoddle as player-manager. He set the foundations and Ruud Gullit and Gianluca Vialli carried this on with Chelsea, winning a number of trophies which rival fans conveniently forget to mention. This book will take you back to the significant games and the childhood memories I have from a truly fantastic Chelsea era. The Hoddle, Gullit & Vialli Years.

1993 - 1994

Glenn Hoddle's arrival at Stamford Bridge as our new player-manager was a huge boost in the summer of 1993. With Ian Porterfield being sacked midway through the 1992/93 season and ex-blue David Webb taking charge for the rest of that season a big appointment was due with the club needing a new direction. Glenn had just won promotion to the Premier League with Swindon Town via the play offs as player-manager and it was now a perfect opportunity for him to take the step up with Chelsea. Glenn stated in his programme notes on the opening game against Blackburn.

"My aim is to be as successful as I possibly can. The club has not had much success recently and I will be trying to help us win some silverware. But it is important how we get success. I wouldn't want to get it by playing dreadful football. The principle of winning by playing good football means a great deal to me".

Most notable was Glenn's first addition as Chelsea manager. Gavin Peacock, a £1.25m signing from Newcastle United was a very exciting prospect having made a big impact in the North East. Gavin could play as an attacking midfielder or striker who quickly became a Chelsea favourite.

Mark Stein signed later on in the season from Stoke City for £1.5m to boost the Chelsea attack. During this season Mark broke a Premier League record by scoring in seven consecutive league matches which was vital as the club flirted at times with the relegation places.

Chelsea finished the season three places lower than they had the previous one in fourteenth position. This however doesn't tell the whole story. A fantastic F.A Cup run saw Chelsea reach the Final for the first time since 1970 and the club were now being noticed. The football was much better to watch with Glenn implementing his own style.

There were certainly some great games during this transitional debut season under Glenn's leadership and the fans continued to feel very optimistic.

The Makita International Soccer Tournament 1993
Date: Sunday 1st August 1993
Result: Chelsea 4-0 Tottenham Hotspur
Chelsea Goal Scorers:
Cascarino (13, 31, 52), Peacock (39)
Venue: White Hart Lane
Attendance: 12,780
Chelsea Team:
Hitchcock, Clarke, Dow, Hoddle (Pearce 81), Johnsen, Lee, Donaghy, Spencer, Cascarino (Shipperley 69), Peacock, Wise

With the new season nearing and mixed pre-season results Chelsea were to play in the Makita Tournament along with Tottenham, Ajax and Lazio with the competition taking place at White Hart Lane. Chelsea's opening game against Ajax finished in a 1-1 draw but saw Chelsea victorious in the penalty shootout. The following day Chelsea played Tottenham in the final as they had beaten Lazio to progress. With Glenn Hoddle now in the Chelsea hot seat despite it only being pre-season it was all set up to be a cracker on a hot summer's day.

Chelsea dominated the final from the very start of the match. After half an hour Chelsea were already 2-0 up with a brace from Tony Cascarino. New signing Gavin Peacock made it 3-0 shortly before half-time and Cascarino completed his hat-trick early in the second-half and that's how it finished. Chelsea won the Makita Tournament beating Tottenham 4-0 and the player of the Tournament was of course Glenn Hoddle.

If anyone was ever sceptical about Glenn's connections with Tottenham this was put firmly to bed before the season even started with this thumping victory.

Chelsea's first game of the new Premier League season was at home to Blackburn Rovers, there was a feel good factor as the Stamford Bridge faithful welcomed Glenn Hoddle. It was the biggest opening day gate at Stamford Bridge for fifteen years, however the result was disappointing. Gavin Peacock scored on his Chelsea debut however defensive mistakes allowed Blackburn to capitalise and win the game 2-1. A draw at Wimbledon and then a 1-0 defeat at Ipswich had fans realising it was going to take time for Glenn to implement his way of playing. Things did pick up after the Ipswich game with a 2-0 home victory against West London neighbours Queens Park Rangers and draws at home to Sheffield Wednesday and away to Tottenham. After the Tottenham game there was an international break with Chelsea not playing for ten days. Next up was Manchester United at Stamford Bridge.

Premier League
Date: Saturday 11th September 1993
Result: Chelsea 1-0 Manchester United
Chelsea Goal Scorer:
Peacock (17)
Venue: Stamford Bridge
Attendance: 37,064
Chelsea Team:
Kharine, Donaghy, Dow (Hall 83), Sinclair, Clarke, Peacock, Kjeldbjerg, Newton, Hoddle, Wise, Cascarino (Shipperley 45)

I went to this game with my dad and it was one of my fondest memories of being in The Shed. We always used to get there about an hour before kick off to get a good spot. I wonder now how accurate the attendances were in those days as most of my visits to Chelsea back then were standing in The Shed and like many other children getting in for free being told to go under the turnstile. Once in the ground the atmosphere was building gradually, I remember my dad chatting to a guy standing next to us who had just returned to the country having being given time off from the army. He was an Irish guy who told his wife that he was returning two days later than what he actually was. He said he had to come and watch his beloved Chelsea and was just praying she didn't see him on Match Of The Day! Although I caught the back end of The Shed days they do hold fantastic memories. The atmosphere, the smell of hot dogs, burgers with cars parked in front and it would always make me laugh when an announcement was made in the stadium that someone's wife had just gone into labour! There was never an expectation for Chelsea to win but when we did it was superb.

Results had been indifferent up until this point and it is never an easy game against Manchester United. Chelsea were always going to have to ride their luck if they were to get the three points.

After a long ball from Glenn Hoddle it was headed clear by Steve Bruce only into the path of Steve Clarke who hit a ferocious shot that Peter Schmeichel could only parry away. Gavin Peacock was the quickest to react and lifted the ball over the outrushing Schmeichel into the back of the net.

Manchester United had chances in the game and the one I remember the most was Eric Cantona turning on the half volley on the half way line and shooting. With Kharine off his line the ball bounced, hit the crossbar and landed safely in Dmitri's hands. It was a massive three points and showed we could more than hold our own against the top teams.

A 1-1 draw at Coventry in the Premier League was followed by a hard-fought 1-1 draw in the first leg of the League Cup away at West Bromwich Albion. The next game was Liverpool at Stamford Bridge.

Up until this game I had now watched Chelsea a handful or so of times, I must say not with great success! It must have been around mid September when my dad said to me 'do you fancy going to the Chelsea v Liverpool game in a couple of weeks?' I was obviously buzzing and replied with an emphatic 'YES!!!' He said, 'that's good, but there's one other thing.' I asked 'what's that then?' he said 'would you like to be the mascot for the day?' I couldn't believe what he had just told me. I was overjoyed that I was about to meet all my Chelsea heroes and lead the team out onto the pitch with Dennis Wise!!!!!! We had three tickets in the director's box and the day would be shared with obviously my dad and my eldest brother Steve. Despite all of Chelsea's success in recent years which I feel very privileged to have been part of, this day remains my greatest day as a Chelsea supporter. I remember soon after being told about this I attempted to sell my Gameboy in order to raise some money to be spent in the club shop on the day. A notice soon went up in our local corner shop and I managed to get £40! On the day itself I was excited and quite nervous at the same time. Playing Liverpool was never going to be easy and a win would just top off a perfect day.

Premier League
Date: Saturday 25th September 1993
Result: Chelsea 1-0 Liverpool
Chelsea Goal Scorer:
Shipperley (48)
Venue: Stamford Bridge
Attendance: 31,271
Chelsea Team:
Kharine, Sinclair, Donaghy (Hall 58), Dow, Clarke, Kjeldbjerg, Newton, Hoddle, Wise, Cascarino, Shipperley

We went for an early pizza down the Fulham Road before heading to the club shop to buy souvenirs to get signed. We quickly made our way to the main reception where I was greeted with a programme (which I was in) and a replica home kit. I was excited! Once I was changed and into my kit we headed to the dressing room to meet the players.

Before we went in we had a quick chat with Glenn Hoddle and Peter Shreeves who were in an adjacent room clearly talking tactics. Glenn then asked me if I was going to bring the team luck today. I obviously replied 'yes'. As we walked into the dressing room it appeared very relaxed and good humoured. My dad actually brought along his video camera which we have some great footage with John Spencer mainly being the joker among the pack. We met all the players and got photos as well as signed footballs and autographs. When meeting Dennis Wise my brother Steve (14 at the time) came out with an absolute classic, 'You playing today Dennis?' His reply was, 'I hope so'. Dennis was obviously club captain. Once we had met all the players it was time for me to take to the famous Stamford Bridge pitch where I had a kick about with the one and only Stamford The Lion. I scored a few penalties against him in front of a few fans who had chosen to get a good spot in The Shed as supposed to being in the pub. From the age of ten I could always say that I scored at Stamford Bridge. As I finished scoring goals past Stamford I joined the players warming up and I remember kicking the ball around with Dennis Wise and Andy Dow. Shaking hands with Dmitri Kharine before returning to the changing rooms praying he would keep a clean sheet. As the players made their final preparations I was asked to wait in the tunnel for Dennis Wise to meet me. I then led the team out in front of 30,000 plus Chelsea fans, a packed Stamford Bridge with The Shed belting out 'Glenn Hoddle's blue and white army'.

As the referee met with the captains (Dennis Wise & Ian Rush) my dad was still on the pitch with his video camera (he wasn't allowed to). Once the coin had been tossed to decide who was shooting which way in the first-half we lined up and at that point I think the officials and players thought my dad was Chelsea's photographer who we later realised didn't turn up to work. The officials quickly made it clear to my dad that he needed to get off the pitch quickly as they had a game to start! The referee gave me the 10p piece that he had made the toss with and I jogged off the pitch. My dad and brother Steve were by the tunnel and we were quickly taken up to our seats in the director's box.

What I actually remember from the game itself is very little as there was so much going on throughout the day. Looking back on the footage of the match I was reminded that we were very fortunate and Liverpool had many chances and probably should have won the game. Fortunately for me it was Chelsea who won the match 1-0 with an early second-half strike from Neil Shipperley. The referee confirmed that the ball had crossed the line after a fumble by Liverpool goalkeeper Bruce Grobbelaar. We hung on for the win but at the time it was a massive three points for us. We actually didn't win another league game after this until December 28th!

After the game I got to meet the goal scorer Neil Shipperley and chairman Ken Bates. It was a similar game to Manchester United, and it was becoming a bit of a thing that Chelsea could win against big teams but would sometimes struggle against teams we were expected to beat. Chelsea were now up to twelfth in the league table with nine games played.

It was thought by many fans that Chelsea would really kick on in the Premier League, six points out of six after beating Manchester United and Liverpool at home. Unfortunately this was not the case.

A 1-0 loss at West Ham wasn't helped with Dennis Wise being sent off shortly after West Ham took the lead. It was always going to be difficult playing the second-half with ten men. Dennis did redeem himself by scoring both goals in a 2-0 victory over West Bromwich Albion in the second round, second leg of the League Cup.

Chelsea were now in their most difficult part of the Premier League season. Defeats to Norwich, Aston Villa, Oldham, Leeds and Arsenal left many journalists debating that Chelsea could possibly be relegated. Chelsea also exited the League Cup losing 1-0 away to Manchester City. Mark Stein made his debut in the 1-0 home defeat to Oldham Athletic and the £1.5m fee from Stoke City would soon be paid back. The lack of goals from Chelsea at this point was seriously concerning, Mark's arrival was very much welcomed.

A 2-0 home defeat to Arsenal was followed by a poor 0-0 draw at home to Manchester City which saw Chelsea's last game in front of the north terrace which was demolished soon after. Defeats to Sheffield United, Blackburn and Southampton with a draw against Ipswich saw Chelsea in a desperate situation sitting second from bottom having played twenty games just after Christmas. Mark Stein opened his

BLUE DAYS

Chelsea account in the 3-1 defeat to Southampton, next up was a huge game at Stamford Bridge the very next day against fifth placed Newcastle.

Premier League
Date: Tuesday 28th December 1993
Result: Chelsea 1-0 Newcastle
Chelsea Goal Scorer:
Stein (11)
Venue: Stamford Bridge
Attendance: 22,133
Chelsea Team:
Kharine, Johnsen, Sinclair, Dow, Clarke, Newton, Burley, Peacock (Spackman 72), Wise, Stein, Shipperley (Spencer 82)

The games were coming thick and fast over the festive period and this particular game was arguably the most important league fixture of the season for Chelsea. Losing how we did the day before at The Dell was very concerning and despite it only being half way through the season there was much talk of relegation amongst the supporters. This was a must win game!

It would be Mark Stein who scored the vital goal after just eleven minutes after some clever play from captain Dennis Wise. A goal riffled in that sparked wild celebrations. Our defence were superb on the day and much thanks had to go to Dmitri Kharine who saved three one-on-one's and denied Newcastle from scoring since the opening day of the season. We climbed out of the bottom three that day with a huge sigh of relief!

Chelsea followed up the great victory with a 3-1 win at relegation favourites Swindon Town. Mark Stein, Dennis Wise and Neil Shipperley amongst the goals to relieve some pressure. A 4-2 victory at home to Everton made it three wins on the spin and Chelsea were finally finding some form.

Attentions then turned to the F.A Cup. A third round tie was remembered as the 'Hoddle derby' as Glenn's brother was playing for our opponents Barnet. It was probably a game Chelsea could have done without as focus was still securing survival in the Premier League. The game was meant to be an away match for Chelsea, however it was agreed that the game would be played at Stamford Bridge. A 0-0 draw meant a replay.

1-1 draws back-to-back in the Premier League away at Norwich and at home to Aston Villa saw Mark Stein scoring both goals to keep his fantastic run going, he'd now rippled the net in six consecutive top flight matches. Chelsea's unwanted F.A Cup third round replay against Barnet came in-between those games. We ran out comfortable winners 4-0 with Craig Burley, Gavin Peacock, Neil Shipperley and Mark Stein with the goals. It would be another F.A Cup replay for Chelsea in the fourth round after a 1-1 draw against Sheffield Wednesday. I remember at the time thinking these replays were really something Chelsea could do without, Gavin Peacock scored Chelsea's goal.

Early February would see Chelsea back in the Premier League away at Everton. A disappointing 4-2 defeat but remembered for Mark Stein scoring two goals, it was then he broke the Premier League goal scoring record by hitting the back of the net in seven consecutive matches.

Back to the F.A Cup and it was a trip to Hillsborough in a fourth round replay. Chelsea weren't expected to win this one and shocked a few with an emphatic 3-1 victory. John Spencer, Craig Burley and Gavin Peacock were amongst the goals in the extra-time win. Chelsea were drawn away to Oxford United in the fifth round and there was a strong feeling that we could continue this cup run into the Quarter-finals.

A disappointing 2-1 defeat away to Oldham saw Chelsea fall down to eighteenth position. The F.A Cup run was positive but it also appeared detrimental to our league form. Chelsea won 2-1 at Oxford in the fifth round thanks to goals from Craig Burley and John Spencer. It was no surprise as Oxford were sitting bottom of the First Division

(Championship). It was however a great feeling that if we could now beat Wolves at Stamford Bridge in the quarter-final we would be off to Wembley! Next up was Tottenham at Stamford Bridge in the league and what a cracker it was!

Premier League
Date: Sunday 27th February 1994
Result: Chelsea 4-3 Tottenham Hotspur
Chelsea Goal Scorers:
Donaghy (29), Stein (33, 90 (pen), Spencer (40)
Tottenham Goal Scorers:
Sedgley (17), Dozzell (18), Gray (73 pen)
Venue: Stamford Bridge
Attendance: 19,398
Chelsea Team:
Kharine, Donaghy, Johnsen, Kjeldbjerg, Clarke, Peacock, Newton, Burley (Hopkin 88), Wise, Stein, Spencer

From the moment I started following Chelsea I always knew the rivalry with Tottenham and to be honest that hasn't changed amongst another generation. I didn't attend this one but in hindsight I wish I did! It's still one of those games that fans still talk about today. The game was however live on television.

Tottenham started the match more brightly than Chelsea and were 2-0 up inside the first twenty minutes scoring two goals within a minute. Pure dejection at this point with the feeling things would probably get worse. However, Mal Donaghy pulled one back thanks to a fortunate deflection and four minutes later Mark Stein equalised with a great shot after Jakob Kjeldbjerg had headed down to him from a Wise corner. Chelsea took the lead for the first time in the match five minutes before half-time with John Spencer riffling into the roof of the net after a great ball from Wise. Chelsea 3-2 up at half-time and you could barely catch your breath.

Erland Johnsen gave away a penalty after handling the ball in the penalty area with Gray equalising.

Tottenham were then awarded another penalty conceded by Dmitri Kharine, he soon redeemed himself by saving it from Gray.

As the game looked as if it would end in a draw as it entered stoppage time it was Chelsea's turn to be awarded a penalty. Some fantastic skill from John Spencer who laid it off to Gavin Peacock, just as he was about to shoot on goal he was fouled by Dean Austin.

Mark Stein stepped up despite Dennis Wise being back in the team. Stein absolutely smashed it into the top left hand corner in front of The Shed. Chelsea won 4-3, it was an absolute thriller at Stamford Bridge.

Next up was a trip to Old Trafford.

Premier League
Date: Saturday 5th March 1994
Result: Manchester United 0-1 Chelsea
Chelsea Goal Scorer:
Peacock (65)
Venue: Old Trafford
Attendance: 44,745
Chelsea Team:
Kharine, Clarke, Johnsen, Kjeldbjerg, Sinclair, Burley, Newton, Peacock, Wise, Spencer, Stein (Hopkin 87)

Manchester United were running away with the league and were also still in the F.A Cup, their last league defeat was when we beat them at Stamford Bridge 1-0 in the September. Chelsea defended heroically in the match with Frank Sinclair back in the team, it was on sixty-five minutes when the breakthrough came. Craig Burley's cross was nodded down by Mark Stein into the path of Gavin Peacock who lobbed the ball over Peter Schmeichel. A 1-0 win and that man Peacock again with the winner. A fantastic result and performance with the only down side Mark Stein going off with an ankle problem late on in the game. Confidence was high going into the F.A Cup Quarter-final against Wolves.

After two fantastic victories in the league against Tottenham and Manchester United our attentions moved back to the F.A Cup. Beating Wolves 1-0 in front of a packed Stamford Bridge was massive with the club reaching the F.A Cup semi-finals for the first time in twenty-four years. It was Gavin Peacock who scored the vital goal showing great quality and the victory sparked a pitch invasion. With the semi-final draw straight after live on television Chelsea found out it would be either West Ham or Luton Town we'd face at Wembley.

A 2-0 victory over Wimbledon secured three league wins on the bounce but fell short losing 2-1 at Liverpool three days later. Soon we'd be back to winning ways in the league after beating West Ham 2-0 at Stamford Bridge with Glenn Hoddle on the score sheet. West Ham also lost to Luton Town the previous Wednesday in the F.A Cup sixth round replay. Chelsea's league form was now very inconsistent losing 3-1 at Sheffield Wednesday. Minds were clearly on the exciting F.A Cup semi-final with Luton at Wembley. League games at home to Southampton and away to Newcastle were to be played before that.

Premier League
Date: Saturday 2nd April 1994
Result: Chelsea 2-0 Southampton
Chelsea Goal Scorers:
Spencer (45), Johnsen (80)
Venue: Stamford Bridge
Attendance: 19,801
Chelsea Team:
Kharine, Clarke, Johnsen, Kjeldbjerg, Sinclair, Burley, Hopkin (Cascarino 45), Newton, Peacock, Wise, Spencer (Barnard 85)

When I was the mascot against Liverpool you'll remember me saying that the official club photographer didn't turn up to work on the day. I had such an amazing time it didn't even register with me. My dad received a letter from the club apologising for this and invited us back to a game at a later date to meet the players and have complimentary tickets for a match. That game was this one, Southampton at home. I remember meeting the mascot and I got to warm up with the players before the game. Straight away Dennis Wise remembered me and said 'Are you the mascot again?' I explained the situation to Dennis and he was probably sick of the sight of me as during this time me and my dad would often sneak into the players bar after games and meet the players.

It was a game that saw both Dave Beasant and Ken Monkou return to Stamford Bridge with Southampton and the Stamford Bridge crowd gave them a warm welcome. Southampton were still battling relegation but they were a bogey team of ours having already beaten us 3-1 just after Christmas. John Spencer scored Chelsea's first settling a few nerves and Erland Johnsen headed the second to secure the win. It was Erland's first goal for Chelsea since his arrival in 1989, a very welcomed three points.

A changed team played in the 0-0 draw at Newcastle as no risks were to be taken ahead of the F.A Cup semi-final.

F.A Cup Semi-final
Date: Saturday 9th April 1994
Result: Chelsea 2-0 Luton Town
Chelsea Goal Scorer:
Peacock (13 & 47)
Venue: Wembley Stadium
Attendance: 59,989
Chelsea Team:
Kharine, Clarke, Johnsen, Kjeldbjerg, Sinclair, Burley (Barnard), Newton, Peacock, Wise, Cascarino, Spencer

This game was my first visit to the old Wembley, as you can imagine at ten years old I was really excited. With Glenn Hoddle at the helm you could feel a new era developing at Chelsea.

I remember going to the game with my dad and brother Steve and feeling quite confident despite Luton's impressive cup run. On the way to Wembley I remember being on the tube and the Chelsea fans going crazy singing songs and shaking the train. I did, if I'm honest feel a little uneasy as it was very loud and something I wasn't used to. Although we had seats on the tube I started to feel much better when a Chelsea fan approached me as he could see I was worried. He had lots of pin badges on his hat and he said I could pick one to keep, very kind of him to do this and I've always remembered this moment.

As we approached Wembley Park station you could really feel the atmosphere building and Chelsea were in full voice which carried on into the ground.

It was Gavin Peacock who opened the scoring on thirteen minutes. A deep cross headed on by Tony Cascarino and then John Spencer. The ball landed to Peacock in the box unmarked who tucked it in the corner from close range.

Steve Clarke shortly after went on a great run with a burst into the box but couldn't convert. Chelsea very much dominated the first-half and captain Dennis Wise also had a great chance to make it 2-0 shortly before half-time.

Chelsea continued to dominate in the second-half and it was Gavin Peacock who made it 2-0 with a tidy finish after a great pass from John Spencer.

After a neat one two between Wise and Spencer with the ball eventually crossed into the path of Cascarino who failed to score from close range. Peacock had another great chance for his hat-trick but his shot was well saved.

The game will always be remembered for two goals from Gavin Peacock and Chelsea legend Kerry Dixon playing for Luton. Kerry received a fantastic reception with 'There's only one Kerry Dixon' echoing around Wembley. A superb day with Chelsea now in the F.A Cup Final.

Frustratingly enough it was very close to being a Chelsea v Oldham

Athletic final if it wasn't for a late Mark Hughes volley that forced a replay. Manchester United won the second game comfortably and it would be them who Chelsea would face. Points however were still needed in the Premier League although from a supporter's point of view it was difficult to think about anything other than the cup final. League results continued to be indifferent with Chelsea drawing 1-1 at QPR, losing 1-0 at Arsenal, drawing with Leeds at The Bridge, beating Swindon 2-0 (Peacock and Wise), drawing 2-2 at Maine Road and then losing at home to Coventry 2-1. The biggest positive coming out of those results was Manchester United won the league on the night of our 2-0 victory over Swindon. Why was that good you may ask? It meant that whatever the result in the F.A Cup Final Chelsea would be playing European football for the first time since 1971 in the form of the European Cup Winners Cup. The last game of the Premier League season would see Chelsea play Sheffield United at Stamford Bridge.

Premier League
Date: Saturday 7th May 1994
Result: Chelsea 3-2 Sheffield United
Chelsea Goal Scorers:
Kjeldbjerg (58), Stein (76 & 90)
Sheffield United Goal Scorers:
Flo (29), Hodges (60)
Venue: Stamford Bridge
Attendance: 21,782
Chelsea Team:
Kharine, Clarke, Johnsen, Kjeldbjerg, Sinclair, Burley (Hoddle 62), Newton, Peacock, Wise, Spencer, Stein

Chelsea trailed 1-0 after a cross from the right was eventually met by Jostein Flo on the half volley as Chelsea failed to clear the danger. Chelsea equalised when a cross from Dennis Wise was met by Danish defender Jacob Kjeldbjerg to score his only goal of the season.

Just two minutes later Sheffield United were 2-1 up. Glyn Hodges came in round the back after a long ball over the top, he managed to knee the ball past the outrushing Kharine.

Chelsea were back on level terms with an equaliser from Mark Stein after some good passing outside the box and a clever lay off from Gavin Peacock. Another great cross from Dennis Wise was helped on into the path of Mark Stein who scored at the far post in injury time.

Chelsea won the game 3-2 and Stein's injury time winner relegated Sheffield United as they fell into the bottom three for the first time with other results going against them.

It was mixed emotions on the day at Stamford Bridge, great to win our final league game of the season and much excitement around the place for the upcoming F.A Cup Final the following week. However, there was a sombre feel as we said goodbye to The Shed. Demolition work would soon start and temporary seating would be put in place for the start of the following season.

The build-up to the F.A Cup Final against Manchester United was so exciting with tickets virtually impossible to get for many. Chelsea were in their first F.A Cup Final for twenty-four years and were the clear underdog even though we were the only team to beat them home and away in the league. Despite Manchester United winning the league there was a thought that we could do it! Chelsea released their traditional F.A Cup Final song in the form of 'No one can stop us now'. As Manchester United's dominance grew in the early 1990's many neutral supporters were hoping Chelsea would go on to lift the F.A Cup.

F.A Cup Final
Date: Saturday 14th May 1994
Result: Chelsea 0-4 Manchester United
Manchester United Goal Scorers:
Cantona (59, 64 x2 pens), Hughes (68), McClair (90)
Venue: Wembley Stadium
Attendance: 79,634

Chelsea Team:
Kharine, Clarke, Johnsen, Kjeldbjerg, Sinclair, Burley (Hoddle 68), Newton, Peacock, Wise, Spencer, Stein (Cascarino 78)

We couldn't get tickets for the Final but I remember watching it at home with the family. We started the game very well and even hit the bar through Gavin Peacock and were unlucky not to go in at half-time 1-0 up. During the second-half Manchester United scored three goals in nine minutes. Two almost identical penalties from Eric Cantona and Mark Hughes with the other. At this point I remember being devastated and our misery was made even worse when Brian McClair scored a fourth late on. The score line was harsh and so were some of the refereeing decisions but sometimes it's the defeats that shape you as a fan.

The next day Chelsea had a parade at Stamford Bridge with many thousands lining the streets in appreciation to our team despite not winning the cup. Me, my dad and older brother Steve were there and I remember feeling very proud to be a Chelsea supporter and couldn't believe so many fans turned up.

This defeat did however mean a European campaign in the Cup Winners Cup the following season. There was still that feeling of how long would it take for Chelsea to get to another major cup final.

Going to school on the Monday was tough, despite living in Essex in the 90's it was a time of Manchester United fans everywhere and very few Chelsea fans. Apart from my brother Steve I think there was only one other Chelsea fan in the whole school. It didn't stop us walking through the school gates proud with our blue and white scarves round our necks.

Losing this final at the time was devastating, the chances of winning a major trophy in those days were very limited and at the time I wondered if Chelsea would ever win anything significant in my lifetime.

BLUE DAYS

Summary of the 1993 - 94 season

A season that will always be remembered for an incredible F.A Cup run that saw Chelsea make it all the way to the final. However, this doesn't tell the full story as Chelsea went on a truly awful run in the Premier League in which we found ourselves second from bottom on December 27th after losing 3-1 at fellow strugglers Southampton. Highs in the Premier League saw Chelsea do the double over eventual champions Manchester United and wins over Liverpool and Tottenham at Stamford Bridge.

The F.A Cup semi-final against Luton Town and the 1-0 victory over Liverpool were my own personal highlights but our league form was very inconsistent. Beating big teams but losing to the likes of Oldham and Sheffield United.

Mark Stein's £1.5m arrival from Stoke City in late October was a stroke of genius from Hoddle as Mark's record of scoring in seven consecutive matches was crucial to the team. Gavin Peacock also had a very good debut season with both players finishing on fourteen goals. Goalkeeper Dmitri Kharine had the most number of appearances making fifty-one in all competitions and special mentions go to captain Dennis Wise, Steve Clarke, and John Spencer who also had positive seasons.

Chelsea's player of the year was Steve Clarke with Glenn Hoddle stating he was 'playing the best football of his career'.

After our final game of the Premier League season in the 3-2 victory over Sheffield United we said a sad goodbye to The Shed.

Despite losing the F.A Cup Final thousands turned out for an open top bus parade around the streets of Fulham. It showed how proud we were of our team and despite indifferent league performances our cup run is one we'll never forget. Players and fans alike were looking forward to the club competing in the European Cup Winners Cup.

1994 - 1995

There was still plenty of optimism in and around Stamford Bridge despite our indifferent league form. Fans were warming towards Glenn Hoddle and the attractive football philosophy he was trying to implement. As Manchester United won the domestic double, Chelsea as F.A Cup runners up would compete in the European Cup Winners Cup which was a very exciting prospect for the players and fans.

During the summer of 1994 there were some departures as well as some new arrivals. Most notably Paul Elliot retired through injury after that horror tackle from Liverpool's Dean Saunders in a clash at Anfield two years previously. A knee injury that he couldn't recover from was such a shame as he was a vital player for Chelsea at the time. We also said goodbye to Steve Livingstone, Damian Matthew, Tony Cascarino and Mal Donaghy who all found new clubs.

Three players came in to bolster Glenn Hoddle's squad and with European football on the horizon squad depth would be vital, especially with UEFA's rule of having only three foreign players in the starting eleven. Striker Paul Furlong was signed from Watford for a club record £2.3m, defender Scott Minto joined from Charlton Athletic and later in the summer midfielder David Rocastle joined from Manchester City for £1.25m. The most notable departure was striker Neil Shipperley who joined Southampton in January 1995 for £1.2m.

Stamford Bridge was also having big redevelopments with a new temporary south stand as The Shed was pulled down. We would also see the new North Stand be unveiled during the 1994/95 season.

Another notable change was that Chelsea's sponsorship with Commodore / Amiga had come to an end. A new deal saw Chelsea begin the season with American lager giants Coors. The home kit remained the same as before with the sponsor being the only difference.

The club felt that with three kits being released in the previous season they wanted to release an away kit that wouldn't clash with any other team. Umbro didn't fail with the attempt and Chelsea released the very much 'marmite' tangerine and graphite kit.

Pre-season results were positive building up to the Makita Tournament taking place at Highbury. Most notably beating Kingstonian 10-0 (I do miss those games). We didn't win the Makita Tournament this time around having lost our first game to Napoli but winning our second game 1-0 against Atletico Madrid. Playing European opposition in pre-season could only be beneficial for what was about to come.

First game of the season, Norwich City at Stamford Bridge. It's always exciting leading up to a new league season and there was real optimism around The Bridge. The North Stand was coming on great and the noise coming from the temporary South Stand certainly made up for only three sides of the ground being open. Goals from Frank Sinclair and Paul Furlong on his debut secured the opening day win which was rather straight forward on reflection. Next up was a memorable away fixture against Leeds at Elland Road.

Premier League
Date: Saturday 27th August 1994
Result: Leeds United 2-3 Chelsea
Leeds Goal Scorers:
Masinga (4), Whelan (19)
Chelsea Goal Scorers:
Wise (pen, 38), Spencer (61, 88)
Venue: Elland Road
Attendance: 32,212
Chelsea Team:
Kharine, Clarke, Johnsen, Kjeldbjerg, Sinclair, Spackman, Rocastle (Newton 82), Peacock, Wise, Furlong, Spencer

A very poor start to the game from Chelsea looking very disorganised and we found ourselves 2-0 down after just nineteen minutes and it felt an almost impossible task to come back. John Spencer won a penalty which Dennis Wise converted shortly before half-time to give us some hope.

John Spencer made it 2-2 with half an hour remaining after Dennis Wise' quick free-kick was spilled by goalkeeper John Lukic, Spencer was on hand to follow up. As the game was coming to an end it looked like it was heading for a draw. The ball fell to John Spencer on the edge of the box after a poor Leeds clearance and Spencer hit a tame shot on the volley which trickled through John Lukic's legs and rolled in the net. 3-2 to Chelsea, a great result and fantastic comeback.

Next up was a trip to Newcastle with both teams having a 100% record going into the match. In a very open game we lost 4-2. When Dennis Wise was sent off with twenty minutes remaining it was clear we weren't going to get anything out the game. We moved on from this result fairly quickly as five days later Chelsea would be competing in a European match for the first time in 23 years.

European Cup Winners Cup First Round, First Leg
Date: Thursday 16th September 1994
Result: Chelsea 4-2 Viktoria Zizkov
Chelsea Goal Scorers:
Furlong (3), Sinclair (5), Rocastle (54), Wise (69)
Viktoria Zizkov Goal Scorers:
Majoros (35, 42)
Venue: Stamford Bridge
Attendance: 22,036
Chelsea Team:
Kharine, Johnsen, Sinclair, Minto, Wise, Newton, Rocastle (Rix 90), Peacock, Spackman, Spencer, Furlong

The thought of Chelsea playing European football was exciting for all generations. It had been such a long time that it was very new for many of the supporters but just as exciting for my Dad's generation who still reminisce about the successful team of 1970/71.

A very early goal gave us the perfect start, a long-range effort from Jakob Kjeldbjerg could only be spilled into the path of Paul Furlong who made it 1-0 inside three minutes. 'Chelsea are back' echoed around Stamford Bridge. Things got even better just two minutes later with Frank Sinclair scoring a header from a Dennis Wise pin point cross. Chelsea did however get a wake up call as Zizkov came back to make it 2-2 before half-time with the equaliser being a fantastic strike.

Our lead was restored soon after the break with a great lob from David Rocastle after a poor clearance from the goalkeeper. Dennis Wise wrapped up a 4-2 victory with the goal of the night, a long-range effort which went in off the cross bar. A great win but we still had the away leg in Prague to come.

Just three days after our European victory over Zizkov our attention was turned back to the Premier League. A real hangover of a game saw us lose at home to Blackburn. A season where we'd compete in four competitions was always going to prove difficult for our squad. A dull 1-0 home victory in the League Cup second round first leg against Bournemouth was followed by a 1-0 league win at Crystal Palace. The second leg against Viktoria Zizkov was next in the Czech Republic which saw us progress after a 0-0 draw. The only scare was conceding a penalty in the first-half which Dmitri Kharine saved. The League Cup second round second leg saw us beat Bournemouth 1-0 at Dean Court (2-0 on aggregate) with Gavin Peacock scoring on the night. The clean sheets were coming which was impressive and no more so than goalkeeper Kharine. Leicester City were next to visit Stamford Bridge.

Premier League
Date: Saturday 8th October 1994
Result: Chelsea 4-0 Leicester City
Chelsea Goal Scorers:
Spencer (1, 49), Peacock (4), Shipperley (76)

Venue: Stamford Bridge
Attendance: 18,397
Chelsea Team:
Kharine, Clarke, Johnsen, Kjeldbjerg, Sinclair, Rocastle, Peacock, Spackman, Wise (Newton 88), Furlong, Spencer (Shipperley 52)

To say Chelsea started the game brightly would be a huge understatement. It took just 17 seconds for us to take the lead through a headed John Spencer goal from a Dennis Wise cross. Just four minutes on the clock and another Dennis Wise cross found Gavin Peacock who scored a diving header.

John Spencer scored his second of the game shortly after half-time slotting home with composure after holding off a defender. Substitute Neil Shipperley rounded off a good win after some clever build-up play from David Rocastle.

Next up was Arsenal away in the Premier League at Highbury. I attended this game with a school friend and his dad who were Arsenal fans, and strangely enough my dad and brother also attended this game with one of my dad's Arsenal friends. We were sat in different parts of the ground and I remember my dad telling me as an eleven year old that 'if Chelsea score you can't jump up and down like we do at Stamford Bridge'. Obviously we'd always try and sit with our own fans but tickets were offered and we couldn't refuse. The Chelsea supporters were located to my right in the clock end and I genuinely couldn't believe how loud they were shortly before kick off.

Chelsea opened the scoring through Wise after Paul Furlong had nodded down Gavin Peacock's cross. At that moment the Chelsea fans were going crazy and so were many people sitting around me. It was quickly apparent there were many Chelsea fans scattered around in the home ends of Highbury. We were eventually beaten 3-1 and it could have been more to be honest but it is certainly a game that sticks in the memory. When Arsenal scored their third goal a guy behind me said, 'don't worry mate we'll still win the league'. We both looked at each other and started laughing.

The second round of the European Cup Winners Cup saw us drawn against Austria Memphis with the first leg at Stamford Bridge. Throughout this competition changes to the team would have to be made as this European competition at the time would only allow three foreign players in the starting eleven. Austria Memphis came to Stamford to defend which they did very well and it frustrated us. The game finished 0-0 and there was still plenty more to come in the away leg. Before the second leg we faced Ipswich Town at Stamford Bridge in the league and won 2-0, a welcomed relief to gain three points after a European fixture.

A 1-0 defeat saw Chelsea exit the League Cup to West Ham at Upton Park, we gave it a good go and were unlucky in parts of the game. With European football, trying to find consistency in the league and the F.A Cup to come it didn't feel like a big blow at the time. A 1-1 draw at Hillsborough was more than a respectable result with a trip to Vienna just a few days away.

European Cup Winners Cup Second Round, Second Leg
Date: Thursday 3rd November 1994
Result: Austria Memphis 1-1 Chelsea
Austria Memphis Goal Scorer:
Narbekovas (73)
Chelsea Goal Scorer:
Spencer (40)
Venue: Ernest Happel Stadion, Wein, Austria
Attendance: 25,000
Chelsea Team:
Kharine, Hall (Minto 46), Barness, Myers, Johnsen, Wise, Spackman, Rocastle (Hoddle 77), Newton, Spencer, Shipperley

A makeshift team made its way to Vienna for the second leg against Austria Memphis. This particular game is remembered for quite possibly the best Chelsea goal scored in Europe and it was all down to one man.

Five minutes before half-time Chelsea cleared from a corner when John Spencer picked the ball up half way inside in his own half and ran seventy yards before beating the goalkeeper emphatically using Eddie Newton as a decoy. There's a great picture of the Chelsea players celebrating the goal in front of the travelling fans with John Spencer on the floor flat out.

Austria Memphis equalised midway through the second-half but the game finished 1-1 with Chelsea going through on the away goals rule. A fantastic night and always remembered for the brilliance of Spencer.

There was now a break from European football until late February where Chelsea would play a two legged quarter-final tie against Belgian side Club Brugge.

Premier League form was inconsistent, a 2-2 draw at home to Coventry, a 3-1 defeat at Liverpool, a 1-0 win at Nottingham Forest and a 0-0 draw at White Hart Lane proved this, with Chelsea now sitting in eleventh place.

Our next game saw the opening of the new North Stand with Everton visiting Stamford Bridge. This was all thanks to Matthew Harding who had put the money up for the new stand when chairman Ken Bates was calling out for investors. I was at the game that day and was sat in the new North Stand which was fantastic. The atmosphere was electric in the ground but the result was disappointing. The game finished in a frustrating 1-0 defeat.

From game to game it was virtually impossible to predict Chelsea's results and that reflected in our league position. A 1-0 win at Southampton, a disappointing 3-0 defeat at Norwich was followed by a dull 0-0 draw at home to Liverpool which was live on Sky.

Boxing Day saw us lose 3-2 at home to Manchester United in a spirited performance against the champions. Other results over the festive period were a 3-0 defeat at Aston Villa and 1-1 draw at home to Wimbledon on New Year's Eve.

There was some respite from the Premier League in early January with the return of the F.A Cup. A 3-0 win at home to Charlton Athletic was more than welcomed. However, the league form didn't change too much at the start of the year. We were picking up points here and there, draws against Sheffield Wednesday and Ipswich Town were followed by a 2-0 home defeat to Nottingham Forest.

Chelsea faced Millwall at The Den in the fourth round of the F.A Cup. The game finished in a 0-0 draw with a replay needed at Stamford Bridge, before that match Chelsea drew 2-2 away at Coventry.

Millwall coming to Stamford Bridge was always going to be a big game and let's be honest there has never been any love lost between the two teams. With the game at 1-1 after extra-time it was Millwall who were victorious in the penalty shoot out. It was the trouble that made the headlines with many fans entering the pitch at the end of the game. Premier League safety and progression in the Cup Winners Cup were now the priority.

After the F.A Cup disappointment there was no time to dwell with two big London derbies on the horizon. First up was a 1-1 draw at home to Tottenham which was followed by an impressive 2-1 win over West Ham at Upton Park with Mark Stein scoring an absolute beauty.

Three days later Chelsea were heading to Brugge for our Cup Winners Cup quarter-final first leg. We lost the game 1-0 but I always thought like many we still had a good chance with the return leg at Stamford Bridge still to come. Another lacklustre performance after a European game saw us draw 0-0 at home to Crystal Palace. A much improved performance in our next game saw us win 2-1 at Manchester City with Mark Stein scoring a double, but defeat at home to Leeds followed shortly before facing Brugge. The squad was struggling with the demands of playing in Europe and injuries. Despite indifferent league form everyone was up for the Brugge game.

European Cup Winners Cup Quarter-final, Second Leg
Date: Tuesday 14th March 1995
Result: Chelsea 2-0 Club Brugge

Chelsea Goal Scorers:
Stein (16), Furlong (38)
Venue: Stamford Bridge
Attendance: 28,661
Chelsea Team:
Hitchcock, Clarke, Johnsen, Sinclair, Minto (Hall 55), Burley, Peacock, Rocastle (Lee 74), Spackman, Furlong, Stein

A very memorable evening at Stamford Bridge and many will remember we wore our 'marmite' orange and grey kit on the night. Trailing 1-0 from the away leg there was still a feel of optimism that we could do it.

The atmosphere inside Stamford Bridge on the night was electric. We made the perfect start on sixteen minutes, a free-kick by Craig Burley found Paul Furlong who nodded down and Mark Stein put the ball into the back of the net with his knee. Chelsea made it 2-0 seven minutes before half-time. Mark Stein fighting a lost cause on the right hand side near the corner flag managed to cross the ball which was deflected into the path of Paul Furlong who side footed into the net. The game finished 2-0 to Chelsea on a fantastic European night, we were now into the semi-final where we were drawn against Real Zaragoza.

After the European heroics Chelsea were quickly brought back to earth with two disappointing away defeats to Blackburn and QPR. Before our Cup Winners Cup semi-final away tie in Zaragoza we played Newcastle at home in the league. I was at this one sat in the North Stand with my dad. Much discussion was our league form and despite a European semi-final to look forward to we were now dangerously close to getting caught up in a relegation fight, similar to the previous season. Gavin Peacock had put us 1-0 up against his former team but again Chelsea conceded a late equaliser.

The Cup Winners Cup semi-final was next up and Zaragoza really taught us a lesson in European football. We lost the game 3-0 and it was now an incredibly difficult task to overturn the three goal deficit at Stamford Bridge.

A 1-1 draw away to Wimbledon followed by a 2-0 home defeat to Southampton saw us just one point above the drop zone going into a home game against Aston Villa. With it looking unlikely we would progress to the Cup Winners Cup Final our league form desperately needed to improve. We now hadn't won at home in the league since beating Ipswich on October 23rd.

Premier League
Date: Saturday 15th April 1995
Result: Chelsea 1-0 Aston Villa
Chelsea Goal Scorer:
Stein (30)
Venue: Stamford Bridge
Attendance: 17,015
Chelsea Team:
Kharine, Clarke, Johnsen, Lee, Kjeldbjerg (Hall 30), Sinclair, Peacock, Rocastle, Spackman, Furlong, Stein (Spencer 80)

A real sense of relief around Stamford Bridge after a very important three points. It was a similar feeling to beating Newcastle at Stamford Bridge the season before with the same match winner. Paul Furlong played in Mark Stein who stepped inside the defender before hammering home. We certainly came under pressure in this game but the win was the important thing, a great atmosphere that day.

Another clean sheet followed in the league with a good 0-0 draw at Old Trafford. Thoughts were now on the return leg against Real Zaragoza at Stamford Bridge. Chelsea gave it everything but fell short despite winning 3-1 on the night. Moving up the Premier League table was now the priority. This started with a 1-0 win over West London neighbours Queens Park Rangers. Next up was a cracker at Goodison Park.

Premier League
Date: Wednesday 3rd May 1995
Result: Everton 3-3 Chelsea
Everton Goal Scorers:
Hinchcliffe (38), Ablett (50), Amokachi (70)
Chelsea Goal Scorers:
Furlong (29 & 77), Hopkin (51)
Venue: Goodison Park
Attendance: 33,180
Chelsea Team:
Kharine, Clarke, Sinclair, Lee, Minto, Burley (Hoddle 74), Hopkin, Spackman, Peacock, Stein, Furlong

Never an easy game at Goodison Park and a point all but secured our Premier League safety. It was a determined performance with a never say die attitude under Glenn Hoddle. Paul Furlong scored his first brace for Chelsea and was unfortunate not to get his hat-trick. It was also a game where David Hopkin scored his first goal for The Blues, a match we led and then equalised twice, a good point.

The last away game followed with a 1-1 draw at Leicester and the last game of the season saw Chelsea play Arsenal at Stamford Bridge. Arsenal had just lost the European Cup Winners Cup Final to Real Zaragoza. A game where the Chelsea supporters were reminding David Seaman of the stunning goal that was scored against him in the Final. Arsenal were in 11th position and Chelsea were in 12th. A 2-1 Chelsea victory saw us finish above Arsenal thanks to Paul Furlong and Mark Stein. A mid-table finish for The Blues.

Summary of the 1994 - 95 season

The season will be remembered for Chelsea being back in Europe and going all the way to the semi-final stage. John Spencer's solo goal in Vienna and a 2-0 home win against Club Brugge will never be forgotten by fans.

Premier League form again was quite inconsistent and that reflected in a mid-table finish. The football being played had improved and fans still felt under Glenn's leadership we were close to doing something special. New signing Paul Furlong contributed with thirteen goals during his first season and finished joint top goal scorer with John Spencer.

The away comeback win against Leeds was fantastic as were memorable home wins against Leicester City and Arsenal.

Gavin Peacock made the most number of appearances (fifty-one) with some being as captain in the absence of Dennis Wise.

Central defender Erland Johnsen was named player of the year who was solid and reliable throughout.

Disappointments in the League Cup and F.A Cup losing to West Ham and Millwall in the early stages of the season but it was always going to be difficult with our squad trying to compete in Europe.

1995 - 1996

Chelsea fans were optimistic and there was still a feeling we were close to winning a trophy. Glenn had now hung up his boots and was now fully focusing on managing the team.

The summer of 1995 was one fondly remembered by Chelsea fans and a time where many felt was when things really changed at the club. Chelsea were linked with signing world football superstar Ruud Gullit. At the time I remember speaking with my dad about it with such excitement, he obviously played it down and said it was 'paper talk' and Chelsea just wouldn't be able to attract such superstars to the club. I kind of knew that even as a kid but one could dream....

The stories of Ruud signing for Chelsea were denied by the club and then to world football's amazement the transfer was finally confirmed with Ruud signing on a free transfer from Sampdoria as his contract had ended. Glenn Hoddle and managing director Colin Hutchinson met with Ruud and a deal was agreed. Our supporters who were not around during this era may not quite ever understand how significant this signing was. It was such a shock and a huge footballing statement. Everyone was desperate to get 'GULLIT 4' on the back of the new home shirt and the stalls around the ground were quickly selling out of wigs. The anticipation of seeing Ruud gliding around the Stamford Bridge pitch in Chelsea blue with his long black dreadlocks was beyond exciting. Even now Ruud can be thought of by many Chelsea fans as one of the most important and significant signings the club has ever made.

Chelsea's transfer business did not stop there, It wasn't long until we were seeing Glenn Hoddle in the newspaper with Manchester United legend Mark Hughes. Another huge signing for the club and a snip at £1.5m. A centre forward that we most definitely needed who was physical and capable of scoring some fantastic goals. Sir Alex Ferguson once said years later that selling Mark Hughes to Chelsea was one of his biggest mistakes in football. As fans we really had to pinch ourselves as Glenn was now bringing in some top class players. Wing back Dan Petrescu signed later from Sheffield Wednesday for £2.3m and left back Terry Phelan was also brought into Glenn's squad later signing from Manchester City. Chelsea said goodbye to David Hopkin who signed for Crystal Palace.

A 5-0 win at Kingstonian in pre-season was followed by seeing Ruud Gullit and Mark Hughes play for the first time in a 3-1 win at Gillingham with Mark on the score sheet. Other pre-season games included wins against Reading, Torquay, Plymouth and Birmingham. There was also a testimonial for Paul Elliot at Stamford Bridge before the season started.

The build-up to the 1995/96 season was one full of excitement and anticipation. Despite two clean sheets the opening two games were quite underwhelming with 0-0 draws at home to Everton and away to Nottingham Forest. Following that was a 2-0 defeat at Middlesbrough. We went into our fourth league game of the season at home to Coventry City without even scoring a goal. We played well against Coventry and should have won the game after going 2-0 up through Dennis Wise and Mark Hughes but defensive lapses cost us and it finished 2-2. Still looking for our first win of the season it was a trip across London on a Monday night to face West Ham at Upton Park.

Premier League
Date: Monday 11th September 1995
Result: West Ham United 1-3 Chelsea
West Ham Scorer:
Hutchinson (73)
Chelsea Goal Scorers:
Wise (31), Spencer (34, 90),
Venue: Upton Park
Attendance: 19,228

Chelsea Team:
Kharine, Johnsen, Minto, Sinclair, Clarke, Newton, Peacock (Lee 73), Wise, Gullit, Hughes, Spencer

There was a lot of pressure on Chelsea going into the game which was live on Sky Sports on the Monday night after an international break. We were outstanding that evening, Dennis Wise opened the scoring which all started from a fifty yard pass from Ruud Gullit who found Scott Minto. A good cross for Hughes who nodded down for Wise who bravely slotted home. Three minutes later it was 2-0 to Chelsea with John Spencer scoring from outside the box after a slight deflection. Shortly before half-time John Spencer fell to the ground after a challenge with Julian Dicks. As Julian jumped over John his studs came down on his head, very debatable as to whether it was deliberate or not but Dicks certainly had a reputation. John came out for the second-half with a big bandage round his head and still had a big part to play in the match.

West Ham pulled a goal back through Don Hutchinson after Chelsea failed to clear from a corner. After a poor foul on Ruud Gullit from Julian Dicks, Chelsea took a very quick free-kick. John Spencer was brought down by Tim Breaker and we were awarded a penalty. Dennis Wise stepped up but it was saved.

A great performance was finally wrapped up in the last minute. A magnificent assist from Ruud allowed Spencer to side foot into the top corner. A well deserved three points with some great performances from Gullit, Hughes, Wise and of course birthday boy John Spencer.

Things got even better with a comfortable 3-0 home victory over Southampton. Second-half goals from Frank Sinclair, Ruud Gullit and Mark Hughes secured the win on the day the club celebrated ninety years of existence. A 0-0 draw followed away to First Division strugglers Stoke City in the League Cup second round first leg. Just as we thought we were becoming more consistent in the league a surprising 2-0 defeat at Newcastle followed. Next up was a home game against London rivals Arsenal.

BLUE DAYS

Premier League
Date: Saturday 30th September 1995
Result: Chelsea 1-0 Arsenal
Chelsea Goal Scorer:
Hughes (52)
Venue: Stamford Bridge
Attendance: 31,048
Chelsea Team:
Kharine, Johnsen, Sinclair, Myers, Spackman, Burley, Peacock (Newton 82), Wise, Gullit, Hughes, Furlong

I remember being at this game with my dad with much talk before the match being about Ruud Gullit facing fellow Dutchman Dennis Bergkamp. Often a difficult game against Arsenal but we ran out worthy 1-0 winners thanks to a strike from Mark Hughes who was now certainly finding the back of the net. Nigel Spackman was sent off towards the end of the game after an altercation with Martin Keown which resulted in Spackman punching him in the back of the head. Like everyone else I was relived at the time that it didn't impact the result. The Bridge was rocking that day with a great result and performance.

Big disappointment in the League Cup second leg with a 1-0 home defeat to Stoke City. Chelsea impressed in the next league game winning 1-0 at Villa Park thanks to Dennis Wise midway through the second-half. A heavy 4-1 home defeat to Manchester United came next where we were never really in the game. A 0-0 home draw with Sheffield Wednesday where new signing Dan Petrescu was paraded on the pitch before the game was sandwiched in between two away defeats to Blackburn and Leeds before facing Bolton Wanderers at Stamford Bridge.

Premier League
Date: Wednesday 22nd November 1995
Result: Chelsea 3-2 Bolton Wanderers

Chelsea Goal Scorers:
Lee (16), Hall (59), Newton (85)
Bolton Goal Scorers:
Curcic (10), Green (68)
Venue: Stamford Bridge
Attendance: 17,495
Chelsea Team:
Kharine, Hall, Johnsen, Lee, Duberry, Petrescu, Burley (Spackman 75), Newton, Wise, Hughes, Stein (Furlong 70)

Bolton were very much struggling in the league losing all of their away fixtures going into the match. Chelsea were extremely inconsistent and were finding it hard to find the back of the net. Curcic put Bolton ahead early on with a fantastic individual goal but Chelsea quickly replied with unlikely goal scorer David Lee arriving in the box.

The second-half saw another unlikely goal scorer in Gareth Hall who curled one brilliantly into the top corner. Green equalised for Bolton before Eddie Newton scored a close range header with five minutes remaining.

Ken Bates' feud with Matthew Harding was apparent for all to see with Ken banning him from the Director's box for the Tottenham game. The match finished 0-0 with Matthew sitting amongst the supporters. A respectable 1-1 draw at Old Trafford followed thanks to Dennis Wise. Next up was Newcastle at home with the Magpie's top of the league at the time, a 1-0 win with Dan Petrescu scoring his first goal for Chelsea. Ken Bates and Matthew Harding were reunited together in the directors box for this one with smiles all round. A late equaliser from Arsenal denied us a win at Highbury but three points were gained at Maine Road thanks to Gavin Peacock. Boxing Day was a real disappointment losing 2-1 at home to Wimbledon, four days later saw us take on Liverpool at Stamford Bridge.

Premier League
Date: Saturday 30th December 1995
Result: Chelsea 2-2 Liverpool
Chelsea Goal Scorers:
Spencer (8, 45)
Liverpool Goal Scorers:
McManaman (33, 76)
Venue: Stamford Bridge
Attendance: 31,137
Chelsea Team:
Kharine, Clarke, Lee, Duberry, Dow, Petrescu, Gullit, Newton, Wise, Furlong (Peacock 85), Spencer

Despite the Boxing Day defeat form had been very good against some of the top teams. Liverpool was always going to be tough and it was a very entertaining game.

The opening goal came from a great Dan Petrescu cross and John Spencer met the ball brilliantly on the volley, without doubt one of Chelsea's goals of the season. A half volley on the edge of box from Steve McManaman equalised for Liverpool.

A long ball over the top from Eddie Newton just before half-time found John Spencer who fought off a challenge from Steve Harkness and placed the ball into the bottom corner. Another equaliser from Mcmanaman with a shot from outside the box made it 2-2. Spencer came close to a hat-trick as he hit the post, a game of real quality and some fantastic goals. It wasn't the win we wanted but the football being watched was just getting better and better.

The New Year started with an evening game in the league at Queen's Park Rangers with Chelsea mid-table. A last minute winner from Paul Furlong secured a 2-1 victory in the West London derby. My dad went to this game and blagged his way into the players bar after the match. I remember an A4 sized programme on my bed when I woke up which was signed by Matthew Harding, Ray Wilkins (QPR manager) and all the players. I was massively excited and the blow of going back to school after the Christmas holidays was no longer on my mind! Being early January our attention was now turned to the F.A Cup and a visit from high flying Newcastle which was live on BBC 1. After playing so well in the match and taking the lead Newcastle equalised in the last minute after a poor goal kick from Dmitri Kharine. A replay to come but the equaliser felt like we had already been knocked out.

A 1-1 league draw followed at Everton before the F.A Cup third round replay at St James' Park.

F.A Cup Third Round Replay
Date: Wednesday 17th January 1996
Result: Newcastle United 2-2 Chelsea (Chelsea won 4-2 on penalties)
Newcastle United Goal Scorers:
Albert (42), Beardsley (64 pen)
Chelsea Goal Scorers:
Wise (62 pen), Gullit (89)
Venue: St James' Park
Attendance: 36,535
Chelsea Team:
Hitchcock, Petrescu, Duberry, Lee, Myers (Clarke 52), Phelan, Wise, Gullit, Newton, Spencer (Peacock 102), Hughes

Like many Chelsea fans I wasn't feeling too confident going into this replay and conceding late in the manner we did at Stamford Bridge was still hurting. Shortly before half-time Albert made it 1-0 from a deflected free-kick but Chelsea replied on the hour mark through a Dennis Wise penalty after John Spencer had been fouled. Darren Peacock received his second yellow card for his foul on Spencer and was therefore sent off (started to believe again).

Newcastle retook the lead after being awarded a penalty themselves after David Lee was adjudged to have fouled Paul Kitson. As the game was reaching the 90th minute it was Chelsea's turn to equalise at the end. Ruud Gullit popping up in the box to hook it in who ran with Michael Duberry to the Chelsea fans who were ecstatic in the corner.

No goals in extra-time meant a dreaded penalty shootout. First up was Beardsley who hit the crossbar, quickly followed by David Lee who hit it hard straight down the middle. Steve Watson had Newcastle's second penalty saved by Hitchcock whilst Wise placed his in the top corner. John Beresford scored but so did Gavin Peacock. Albert scored his but we only needed to score the next one and we would be through to the fourth round. Up stepped Eddie Newton..... YYYeeeaaahhhhh! Eddie sent the goalkeeper the wrong way as the Chelsea players ran to the travelling fans.

Following on from the dramatic victory at Newcastle it was now back to the Premier League. Just a few days later a 1-0 home win over Nottingham Forest was quickly followed by another game at Stamford Bridge against Middlesbrough.

Premier League
Date: Sunday 4th February 1996
Result: Chelsea 5-0 Middlesbrough
Chelsea Goal Scorers:
Peacock (29, 38, 55), Spencer (31), Furlong (52)
Venue: Stamford Bridge
Attendance: 21, 060
Chelsea Team:
Hitchcock, Phelan, Sinclair (Johnsen 80), Petrescu, Clarke, Lee, Peacock, Newton, Gullit, Spencer (Morris 72), Furlong

A game that was live on television, I remember feeling quite confident going into the match but never did I think it would be so comfortable. Some fantastic goals and a great hat-trick from Gavin Peacock, which was the first from a Chelsea player in five years and the biggest top-flight win for Chelsea in thirty-five years. A seventeen year old Jody Morris made his debut as a second-half substitute in a memorable win that took

Chelsea up to seventh in the league and unbeaten in eight matches.

Two disappointing league defeats followed at struggling Coventry City and at home to London rivals West Ham. A 0-0 draw away to Grimsby Town in the F.A Cup fifth round meant a replay was to come at Stamford Bridge. With no wins in three it was a trip to the south coast.

Premier League
Date: Saturday 24th February 1996
Result: Southampton 2-3 Chelsea
Southampton Goal Scorers:
Widdrington (6), Shipperley (38)
Chelsea Goal Scorers:
Wise (20, 26 pen, Gullit (53)
Venue: The Dell
Attendance: 15,226
Chelsea Team:
Hitchcock, Clarke, Lee, Duberry (Johnsen 71), Petrescu, Phelan, Gullit, Peacock, Spackman (Spencer 80), Wise, Hughes

Disappointingly we fell behind very early in the game after failing to clear from a corner. It wouldn't be long until Dennis Wise equalised with a fantastic long-range shot and then decided to pretty much run the length of the pitch to celebrate with goalkeeper Kevin Hitchcock. It was former blue Ken Monkou who conceded a penalty just six minutes later after fouling Dennis Wise who collected a great ball from Ruud Gullit. Dennis took the penalty and scored past former team mate Dave Beasant. It was certainly a game of former Blues as Neil Shipperley bundled the ball over the line to equalise shortly before half-time. The game was won by a fantastic goal just after the break. Ruud Gullit picked the ball up on the half way line and drove forward, a one two with Mark Hughes before lifting the ball over the outrushing Beasant high into the net. A fully entertaining game with some great Chelsea goals, we were now up to eighth in the league.

BLUE DAYS

Back at Stamford Bridge for the F.A Cup fifth round replay against Grimsby Town, a straight forward 4-1 victory with some great goals on the night. A 1-1 draw followed away to Wimbledon before facing them again seven days later in the F.A Cup quarter-final at Stamford Bridge. The game finished in an entertaining 2-2 draw with another replay to follow. Before we met the Wombles yet again there was still work to be done in the Premier League with two difficult fixtures. A 1-1 draw at home to Manchester City will only be remembered for Ruud Gullit scoring one of the Chelsea goals of the season. A 2-0 defeat at Anfield followed with confidence a little low going into the replay with Wimbledon.

F.A Cup Quarter-final Replay
Date: Wednesday 20th March 1996
Result: Wimbledon 1-3 Chelsea
Wimbledon Goal Scorer:
Goodman (39)
Chelsea Goal Scorers:
Petrescu (20), Duberry (79), Hughes (84)
Venue: Selhurst Park
Attendance: 21,380
Chelsea Team:
Hitchcock, Clarke, Lee, Duberry, Petrescu, Phelan, Burley, Gullit (Furlong 87), Wise, Hughes, Spencer (Peacock 86)

Having school the next day meant still no evening games for me unfortunately. Was actually gutted as my dad was going to the match and with Wimbledon playing at Selhurst Park it always meant the away fans got three sides of the ground. I remember feeling quite nervous for this one and on their day Wimbledon at the time could cause problems for any team. The nerves were quickly disappearing as Dan Petrescu smashed the ball in from an acute angle with twenty minutes on the clock with some of our fans on the pitch. We were completely in control with

Mark Hughes and Ruud Gullit having great shots either side of Dennis Wise missing a penalty. Typically from Wimbledon they equalised five minutes before half-time through their only attempt, the nerves were certainly back for the second-half.

It took Chelsea until eleven minutes from time to get the lead back and it was defender Michael Duberry with a towering header from a John Spencer cross. The tie was all over five minutes later thanks to a great run down the left from Gullit who assisted for an easy finish for Hughes. I remember being absolutely buzzing after this result and it would be Manchester United who we'd face in the semi-final at Villa Park.

Chelsea's inconsistencies were showing with a disappointing 1-1 draw at home to QPR before the semi-final.

F.A Cup Semi-final
Date: Sunday 31st March 1996
Result: Manchester United 2-1 Chelsea
Manchester United Goal Scorers:
Cole (55), Beckham (59)
Chelsea Goal Scorer:
Gullit (35)
Venue: Villa Park
Attendance: 38,421
Chelsea Team:
Hitchcock, Clarke (Johnsen 38), Lee (Furlong 86), Myers, Duberry, Phelan (Peacock 64), Burley, Gullit, Wise, Hughes, Spencer

This game was huge for Chelsea and we certainly travelled to Villa Park in numbers being the only semi-finalist to sell out our full allocation. I remember the build-up to the game and the focus was most certainly on Ruud Gullit and Eric Cantona. We were desperate to overcome the disappointment of 1994 but unfortunately it wasn't meant to be. On reflection it was a very good game with both teams having a number of chances. David Beckham struck the post before Michael Duberry had a cracking shot against the cross bar. Mark Hughes with some great work on the left hand side produced a perfect cross on the half volley which found Ruud Gullit who headed in from close range. Eric Cantona then hit the post shortly before half-time. Andy Cole equalised from close range before David Beckham scored from the right hand side where Terry Phelan was clearly struggling through injury after a poor back pass from Craig Burley. Having already had Dan Petrescu out of the game and Steve Clarke taken off injured in the first-half, Phelan felt he could continue and Manchester United capitalised. Gullit and Spencer were unlucky not to equalise but despite the disappointment we more than competed with them. We knew we were close to winning something but we had to wait just a little bit longer, our fans were class on the day.

An F.A Cup hangover followed with a disappointing home defeat to Aston Villa despite taking the lead. It was ground hog day away to Bolton on Easter Monday with Chelsea taking the lead through Spencer again and losing 2-1. Three defeats in a row now and the prospect of playing Leeds United at Stamford Bridge did not seem appealing.

Premier League
Date: Saturday 13th April 1996
Result: Chelsea 4-1 Leeds United
Chelsea Goal Scorers:
Hughes (19, 35, 48 pen), Spencer (20)
Leeds United Goal Scorer:
McAllister (66)
Venue: Stamford Bridge
Attendance: 22,131
Chelsea Team:
Kharine, Lee, Myers, Duberry, Minto, Burley, Gullit, Spackman, Wise, Hughes, Spencer (Peacock 69)

I remember being at this one with my dad and brother. Always difficult to predict these games especially how inconsistent both clubs had been with the league table reflecting this.

It turned out to be a great afternoon but not for the Leeds defence and goalkeeper John Lukic who had an absolute shocker. Nether the less it was a hat-trick from the returning Mark Hughes and three goals in three games for John Spencer. A great day and pleasing to get back to winning ways.

There was much talk around Glenn Hoddle's future at Chelsea and whether he would sign a new contract. A 0-0 draw at Sheffield Wednesday and a 1-1 draw at Tottenham followed. At the start of May before our last game of the season the news broke that Glenn Hoddle would become the new England manager after Euro '96, becoming Terry Venables' successor. Glenn stated 'it was the only job I would have left Chelsea for'. It was disappointing as we all felt Glenn was on the brink of winning something after such a long wait but understandably it was an opportunity he couldn't turn down. Ken Bates soon announced Glenn's successor and it would now be Ruud Gullit to take the team forward as player-manager.

The season finished with a 3-2 home defeat to Blackburn Rovers however everyone was already looking forward to the next season and eagerly anticipating how we could get on under Ruud. I remember at the end of the final game Glenn received a great ovation and one fan took it upon himself to run on the pitch and kiss Gullit's boots before being escorted away by the stewards. Chelsea finished the league campaign in eleventh position.

Summary of the 1995 - 96 season

Another season that saw Chelsea come very close to winning a long awaited trophy and the thought was it would happen sooner rather than later. The football played was improving all the time and we became much more attractive to watch. There were however inconsistencies in our league form and that was apparent from our eleventh place finish.

A season that saw captain Dennis Wise have the most number of appearances and John Spencer finish as our highest goal scorer. A great debut season for Ruud Gullit and Mark Hughes which saw Ruud win Chelsea's player of the year.

Some memorable games which included league wins over Arsenal, Leeds and a thumping 5-0 against Middlesbrough which saw Gavin Peacock score a Chelsea hat-trick which hadn't been achieved for six years. The win on penalties at Newcastle in the F.A Cup and the 3-1 win at Wimbledon were also very memorable.

With Glenn Hoddle taking the England job all eyes were now firmly on Ruud!

1996 - 1997

It was a very exciting time to be a Chelsea fan and it got even better when Ruud Gullit unveiled Italian super star striker Gianluca Vialli as his first signing on a free transfer from Juventus. A great addition to the squad and an indication as to the quality of players Ruud could attract to the club.

Fellow Italian Roberto Di Matteo followed in a £4.9m transfer from Lazio as did French defender Frank Leboeuf for £2.5m who both signed on the same day. Ruud also brought in fitness coach Ade Mafe to his backroom staff. Of course with new players coming in there was always going to be players leaving the club. Most notably we said goodbye to striker Paul Furlong who signed for Birmingham City for £1.5m and later in the season we would say goodbye to John Spencer, Gavin Peacock and Terry Phelan.

Pre-season kicked off with an emphatic win at Kingstonian and there would be further warm up games against Exeter City, Plymouth Argyle and Swindon Town before participating in the Umbro International Tournament. This tournament was played at the City Ground over a weekend with ourselves, Nottingham Forest, Manchester United and Ajax competing for a pre-season trophy. We drew our first game against hosts Nottingham Forest but won the game 4-3 on penalties which meant we'd face Dutch giants Ajax in the final the following day. Two early goals from Dennis Wise and Dan Petrescu secured the win for Chelsea and fans got to see striker Gianluca Vialli for the first time as we won the trophy wearing the new yellow away kit. Seeing Chelsea win any trophy at this point was a bonus and despite being pre-season this was no different. Little did we know what success was about to come our way.

A win against Sampdoria followed as did a benefit match for club legend Steve Clarke against PSV Eindhoven at Stamford Bridge. There was now no temporary stand in The Shed End as it was boarded up with work on the new development taking place.

Now we were anticipating the start of the season with an opening day fixture away to Southampton. The first game of the Premier League season finished in a 0-0 draw at The Dell, it was somewhat of an anti climax with Chelsea dominating the game but just couldn't find a way through. Gianluca Vialli, Roberto Di Matteo and Frank Leboeuf all made their Chelsea debuts. Just three days later Chelsea would face Middlesbrough in our first league game at Stamford Bridge.

Premier League
Date: Wednesday 21st August 1996
Result: Chelsea 1-0 Middlesbrough
Chelsea Goal Scorer:
Di Matteo (86)
Venue: Stamford Bridge
Attendance: 28,272
Chelsea Team:
Kharine, Clarke, Johnsen, Leboeuf, Petrescu, Minto, Di Matteo, Morris, Wise, Hughes, Vialli

I remember the build-up to this one with much talk of Gianluca Vialli facing Italian teammate and Middlesbrough's new signing Fabrizio Ravanelli. A fantastic atmosphere inside Stamford Bridge saw our new signings take their bow on home turf, Jody Morris started his first Premier League game amongst a host of superstars.

Di Matteo came close to opening the scoring in the first-half only to be denied by a fantastic save. There were half chances at both ends in all honesty and it looked like the game was heading for another 0-0 draw. With four minutes remaining Di Matteo shot from twenty-five yards which found the bottom corner. If you don't remember the goal or the game you will certainly remember the goal celebration, lying down on the pitch raising one arm in the air. Chelsea were up and running with our first three points of the season.

Another home match quickly followed with a 2-0 victory over Coventry City. Both Frank Leboeuf and Gianluca Vialli scored their first goals for the club in a comfortable win.

Premier League
Date: Wednesday 4th September 1996
Result: Arsenal 3-3 Chelsea
Arsenal Goal Scorers:
Merson (44), Keown (64), Wright (77)
Chelsea Goal Scorers:
Leboeuf (6, pen), Vialli (30), Wise (90)
Venue: Highbury
Attendance: 38,132
Chelsea Team:
Kharine, Clarke, Johnsen, Myers, Leboeuf (Duberry 60), Petrescu, Burley (Spencer 83), Di Matteo, Wise, Hughes, Vialli

A dramatic six goal thriller at Highbury showed Chelsea's never die attitude under Ruud Gullit. Taking an early lead through a Frank Leboeuf penalty certainly eased the nerves. On the half hour mark Gianluca Vialli make it 2-0 to everyone's surprise, a fierce shot on the right hand side crept in as John Lukic made a bad mistake. Vialli initially didn't know he had scored as he tumbled as a result of the follow through from his shot. He soon realised as he saw the Chelsea fans in the corner celebrating.

Arsenal pulled one back shortly before half-time and Martin Keown equalised twenty minutes into the second-half. Chelsea were really up against it at this point and a rash decision by Kharine coming way out of his box allowed Ian Wright to score. Looking like it would end in defeat for Chelsea we managed to equalise deep into stoppage time. A great ball over the top by substitute John Spencer found Dennis Wise who smashed home. A hard-fought point which we were all pleased with despite at one stage having a two goal lead.

Sheffield Wednesday away was next in the league which ended in a solid 2-0 victory thanks to Craig Burley and unlikely scorer Andy Myers. It was a great result as Wednesday were top of the league having won their first four matches. Most notably from this game was the significant injury to goal keeper Dmitri Kharine, Kevin Hitchcock replaced him making some fine saves. A 1-1 draw at home to Aston Villa live on Sky was frustrating as we could have gone top with a win, however we were still unbeaten.

Attentions turned to the League Cup second round, first leg with a trip to Blackpool. A comfortable 4-1 victory on the night but a second leg was still to come. Just three days later we certainly came crashing down at league leaders Liverpool. A 5-1 thumping hurt, considering how well we had started the season. It didn't get any better after the Liverpool game losing 3-1 at home to Blackpool in the second leg of the League Cup. It was a scare but we managed to progress 5-4 on aggregate. A 3-1 victory at Leicester City followed a disappointing 1-1 draw at home to Nottingham Forest, conceding in injury time. League inconsistencies were soon apparent again losing 4-2 at home to Wimbledon.

League Cup Third Round
Date: Tuesday 22nd October 1996
Result: Bolton Wanderers 2-1 Chelsea
Bolton Wanderers Goal Scorers:
McGinlay (22), Blake (43)
Chelsea Goal Scorer:
Minto (2)
Venue: Burnden Park
Attendance: 16,867
Chelsea Team:
Hitchcock, Clarke, Johnsen, Leboeuf, Minto (Phelan 76), Burley, Di Matteo, Gullit, Wise, Hughes, Spencer

Bolton were top of the Division below the Premier League and were in fine form going into the cup tie. It was never going to be easy but we took a very early lead through a clever Scott Minto goal, defensive frailties cost us and we lost the game 2-1.

Going to bed that night disappointed with our exit from the League Cup it was school for me the next morning. My older brother Steve informed me in the playground that Matthew Harding had died in a helicopter crash coming back from the game, killing everyone on board. Like everyone else I was in complete shock. A time before the internet and social media I was just hoping he had somehow got it wrong. It was on my mind all day at school with more people talking about the news. At the end of the day I rushed home from school only to see it on the news and left feeling heartbroken.

Premier League
Date: Saturday 26th October 1996
Result: Chelsea 3-1 Tottenham Hotspur
Chelsea Goal Scorers:
Gullit (27), Lee (52 pen), Di Matteo (80)
Tottenham Goal Scorer:
Armstrong (41)
Venue: Stamford Bridge
Attendance: 28,318
Chelsea Team:
Hitchcock, Clarke (Johnsen 59), Lee (Phelan 79), Duberry, Petrescu, Minto, Di Matteo, Gullit (Burley 73), Wise, Hughes, Vialli

The club had decided that our home Premier League game with Tottenham would go ahead just four days later. We had tickets for the match that we bought a few weeks before. We were actually sat in the new, Matthew-Harding-financed, North Stand which was soon to be named after him. It was the most emotional and surreal feeling at a match that I have ever witnessed. All the players wore black armbands and captain Dennis Wise, Steve Clarke and goalkeeper Kevin Hitchcock led the tributes with a large wreath and a pint of Guinness was placed in the centre circle. A very emotional minute silence followed and despite the rivalry Tottenham's fans were extremely respectful throughout the game. Clichéd I know but tragedy in football often brings fans together, once the referee blew his whistle we just wanted three points for Matthew.

As we know it's always a big game against Tottenham but this one just felt different for obvious reasons. Chelsea took the lead and it was quite fitting it was player / manager Ruud Gullit. A header from Mark Hughes came off the post and Ruud was on hand to score cleverly from the rebound.

An unfortunate error from Kevin Hitchcock allowed Tottenham to equalise shortly before half-time through Chris Armstrong. Seven minutes into the second-half Chelsea were awarded a penalty after Dan Petrescu was tripped by Sol Campbell. David Lee stepped up and went for power and Ian Walker was unable to keep it out. David unfortunately broke his leg later in the match after a clash with Campbell. The game was wrapped up ten minutes from time with a tidy finish from Roberto Di Matteo. A great result with Matthew in our thoughts throughout.

In a post match interview Dennis Wise paid tribute to Matthew and followed up by saying, "we've just got to go on and win something for him now and make his dream come true".

Premier League
Date: Saturday 2nd November 1996
Result: Manchester United 1-2 Chelsea
Manchester United Goal Scorer:
May (81)
Chelsea Goal Scorers:
Duberry (31), Vialli (61)
Venue: Old Trafford
Attendance: 55,198

Chelsea Team:
Hitchcock, Clarke, Duberry, Leboeuf, Petrescu, Minto, Burley, Di Matteo, Wise, Hughes, Vialli

Norwegian goalkeeper Frode Grodas joined the club on a free transfer before the game but would not make his debut until the following match.

With a positive result against Spurs in tragic circumstances we had nothing to fear facing Premier League contenders Manchester United. Emotions were still running high which could be seen from Michael Duberry's celebration after a great header from a Dennis Wise corner. Chelsea made it 2-0 with half an hour remaining after a wonderful long ball from Frank Leboeuf set Vialli clear. One-on-one with only goalkeeper Peter Schmeichel to beat Luca placed the ball in between his legs. "When the ball hits the back of the Old Trafford net, it's Vialli, it's Vialli!" A deflected Poborsky shot off David May pulled one back but it wasn't enough as we gained another fantastic three points.

Just six days after the great win at Old Trafford Chelsea announced the signing of Italian forward Gianfranco Zola. A £4.5m signing from Parma was welcomed in front of the media alongside Ruud Gullit. A 1-1 draw at Blackburn saw both goalkeeper Frode Grodas and Gianfranco Zola make their debuts. Another 1-1 draw followed against table toppers Newcastle, was it a home debut goal from Zola or not? The faintest of touches from Gianluca Vialli? Only Luca would know and he was credited with the goal, a game we should have won with the amount of chances we created. A 2-0 defeat at Leeds was disappointing and a draw at The Bridge against Everton followed in another game we should have got three points.

On the day of the Everton match my dad had a dinner dance with his work colleagues with an overnight stay at the Cadogan Hotel in London. My mum and I went with him and my dad tied it in with watching Chelsea in the afternoon. After checking in late morning it was a quick change into my Chelsea shirt before shortly heading off to Stamford Bridge. As my dad was chatting with a receptionist about the arrangements for the dinner / dance I sat in reception. Eager to be on our way a bald headed guy suited and booted with sunglasses on came through the hotel's double doors. It was Gianluca Vialli! I quickly interrupted my dad's conversation and proceeded to approach Gianluca. A quick hello and an autograph on a hotel piece of paper left us even more buzzing for the game.

A match where we had many chances to win but defensive errors cost us. Gianfranco Zola scored his first goal for Chelsea and Vialli scored the equaliser with a bullet header. On the way back to the hotel we purchased a Chelsea shirt with Vialli number nine on the reverse with the hope we could get him to sign it. Back at the hotel we left the shirt with a receptionist, Luca was at that point living at the hotel until he found more permanent accommodation. Whilst my mum and dad got ready for their evening I remember staying in the hotel room watching television and kept looking at Luca's autograph and wondering whether he would sign the shirt we bought. My dad came up a few times to check I was ok and soon it was time for Match Of The Day.

Waking up bright an early the next day I instantly just wanted to see if he had signed the shirt. Once we got downstairs the receptionist straight away came over and said 'Luca was more than happy to sign this for you'. I couldn't believe my luck! Despite not getting the three points it was a great weekend.

Chelsea's inconsistent form at this stage of the season was very apparent as a disappointing 3-0 defeat at Sunderland followed. Next up was a London derby against West Ham at Stamford Bridge.

Premier League
Date: Saturday 21st December 1996
Result: Chelsea 3-1 West Ham United
Chelsea Goal Scorers:
Hughes (6, 35), Zola (10)
West Ham Goal Scorer:
Porfirio (11)

Venue: Stamford Bridge
Attendance: 28,315
Chelsea Team:
Grodas, Clarke, Duberry, Clement (Myers 58), Petrescu, Burley (Sinclair 83), Di Matteo, Gullit, Newton, Hughes, Zola

With Christmas soon approaching the games were piling up with Chelsea suffering from injuries and suspensions. It would be a new strike partnership of Hughes and Zola and they instantly hit it off after just six minutes with Sparky opening the scoring. Franco shortly made it 2-0 with arguably his best goal in a Chelsea shirt, I'm sure Julian Dicks is still spinning! A wonderful individual effort, twisting and turning before smashing the ball home.

Chelsea were cruising only to give away a goal soon after taking a two goal lead. The final goal of the game came ten minutes before half-time. A great cross from Dan Petrescu found Mark Hughes whose header went in off the post. A much needed three points and a very pleasing result and performance.

A great 2-0 victory at Aston Villa followed on Boxing Day with Gianfranco Zola scoring a second-half double. The win was pleasing but so was the much needed clean sheet. A 2-2 draw at home to Sheffield Wednesday felt like a defeat after being 2-0 up, a front two of Hughes and Zola continued to impress with them both getting on the score sheet. New Year's Day saw Liverpool arrive at Stamford Bridge and it wouldn't be the only time we'd face them in January. Never an easy game but Roberto Di Matteo capitalised on a mistake to score the only goal of the game. I was at this match and I remember it being a huge win as Liverpool were top at the time. Ten points from a possible twelve with Chelsea now up to seventh.

Early January saw Chelsea face West Bromwich Albion at The Bridge in the F.A Cup third round. A tie we were expected to win and the only competition that we could potentially win. Dennis Wise, Craig Burley and Gianfranco Zola secured our place in the fourth round where we'd face Liverpool.

A disappointing 2-0 defeat at lowly Nottingham Forest was just a blip as we went on to beat Derby 3-1, with the game remembered for Paul Hughes scoring a great first goal for the club.

All eyes were now on Liverpool in the F.A Cup.

F.A Cup Fourth Round
Date: Sunday 26th January 1997
Result: Chelsea 4-2 Liverpool
Chelsea Goal Scorers:
Hughes (50), Zola (58), Vialli (63, 76)
Liverpool Goal Scorers:
Fowler (10), Collymore (21)
Venue: Stamford Bridge
Attendance: 27,950
Chelsea Team:
Hitchcock, Petrescu, Clarke, Leboeuf, Sinclair, Minto (Hughes 46), Newton, Wise, Di Matteo, Zola, Vialli

This game is often remembered by many Chelsea fans as one of the best ever at Stamford Bridge. I was not at this one but have my own memories of a truly great day. It was actually my dad's 50th birthday, a family occasion celebrating it by going out for a meal but making sure we were back in time for kick off. Live on BBC 1 I remember the whole family surrounding the television in anticipation. Despite beating them on New Year's Day Liverpool were clear favourites to progress to the fifth round with them still looking like title contenders.

We didn't start the game well and found ourselves 2-0 down after just twenty minutes. Liverpool were running riot and should have been at least 3-0 up at half-time. During the break I remember feeling absolutely gutted and the thought of facing Liverpool supporting friends at school the next day left me sick to my stomach. There was absolutely no way we could turn this around and another trophyless season looked apparent.

As the teams came out for the second-half Mark Hughes was ready to come on and it would be Scott Minto that would come off. The whole flow of the game started to change and within five minutes Hughes pulled one back with a clever shot on the turn. Pleased at this point but still more hopeful than confident. A clever lay off from Hughes just minutes later allowed Zola to control the ball and unleash one into the top corner! I couldn't quite believe it, it was a completely different game from the first-half.

Just five minutes later the unthinkable happened, a through ball from Dan Petrescu found Vialli who poked the ball past goalkeeper David James. 3-2! Vialli then went on to score again, a free-kick from Zola and Vialli headed home. A truly unbelievable game and a result we could never have imagined at half-time. A day all Chelsea fans know where they were, and one my dad shares with his 50th birthday. Chelsea would face Leicester in the fifth round with many talking about the possibility of Chelsea winning the cup.

It was now a trip across London to Tottenham in the Premier League. A great 2-1 victory with Chelsea taking the lead after just fifty seconds through an own goal. The points were secured in the second-half after a rocket from Roberto Di Matteo.

An international break followed before Chelsea travelled to Leicester in the F.A Cup. Gianfranco Zola scored the only goal at Wembley as Italy beat England 1-0. Despite Leicester's league position they were often difficult opposition at Filbert Street with Martin O'Neil in charge. Another game live on the BBC saw Chelsea cruising 2-0 thanks to goals from Roberto Di Matteo and Mark Hughes. Disappointingly we let the lead slip conceding two goals from set plays, a tough replay was to come.

Manchester United were next in the league and this game was remembered for a wonderful individual goal from Gianfranco Zola early in the game leaving United players on the floor. An equaliser followed from David Beckham, which no goal keeper would be able to save.

F.A Cup Fifth Round Replay

Date: Wednesday 26th February 1997
Result: Chelsea 1-0 Leicester City (AET)
Chelsea Goal Scorer:
Leboeuf (pen, 116)
Venue: Stamford Bridge
Attendance: 26,053
Chelsea Team:
Grodas, Clarke, Leboeuf, Sinclair, Peterescu (Johnsen 106), Minto (Vialli 45), Di Matteo, Newton, Wise, Hughes, Zola

With school the following day and no sky in our household it was an evening spent in my local community centre bar to watch the game with dad. Looking back I can't remember feeling more nervous for a game. Sat there with a packet crisps and a coke there was that gut-wrenching feeling of how important this replay was. As I said previously Leicester were a team that would never give up and they certainly didn't that night at Stamford Bridge. Chelsea hit the woodwork twice and goalkeeper Kassey Keller made some outstanding saves. Leicester only really threatened in the last minute when Frank Leboeuf had to clear off the line.

The game went to extra-time and later Erland Johnsen replaced the exhausted Dan Petrescu. As it appeared a penalty shootout was on the cards Erland burst forward and attempted a one-two with Vialli. In an amongst limbs Erland went down in the box. He didn't dive but it certainly wasn't a penalty. The Leicester players were furious however Dennis Wise didn't need any encouragement to defend his team mate. Frank Leboeuf coolly stepped up and sent Keller the wrong way. The final whistle soon blew with a huge sigh of relief, we were now in the F.A Cup quarter-final where we'd play Portsmouth at Fratton Park.

With supporters minds focused on the F.A Cup inconsistent league results soon followed. A 3-2 defeat at Derby also saw Frank Leboeuf sent off and Ruud Gullit break his ankle, which ruled him out for the remainder of the season. Blackburn at home was our sixth game in seventeen days which ended in a 1-1 draw. Attentions turned back to the F.A Cup where we played First Division Portsmouth away, a solid 4-1 victory with Hughes, Zola & Wise (2) on the score sheet. Chelsea would now face Wimbledon in the semi-final at Highbury. Another 3-2 away defeat in the league followed, this time at West Ham and another last minute winner. Next up was Sunderland at Stamford Bridge live on Sky.

Premier League
Date: Sunday 16th March 1997
Result: Chelsea 6-2 Sunderland
Chelsea Goal Scorers:
Zola (38), Sinclair (43), Petrescu (52), Hughes (77, 89), Di Matteo (90)
Sunderland Goal Scorers:
Stewart (58), Rae (60)
Venue: Stamford Bridge
Attendance: 22,762
Chelsea Team:
Grodas, Clarke, Myers (Parker 66), Sinclair, Petrescu, Minto, Burley, Di Matteo, Wise, Hughes, Zola (Vialli 84)

A much lower crowd at this one, with it gaining sky coverage and being on a Sunday (which was then a rarity) it perhaps put some off. However, the supporters who did go were in for a treat.

Two quick Chelsea goals shortly before half-time put The Blues in cruise control. A Petrescu cross was volleyed in perfectly by Zola and soon after Zola turned provider for Frank Sinclair to head downwards for a 2-0 lead. Shortly after the re-start it was 3-0 with Dan Petrescu following up a shot from Zola which was initially saved. Chelsea were however leaking goals and this game was no different. Sunderland managed to score two goals in as many minutes with our defensive frailties still apparent.

Our nerves were made a lot easier though after a great individual goal from Mark Hughes made it 4-2. Substitute Vialli with some great work on the right hand side provided Hughes with an easy tap-in as we approached ninety minutes. There was still however time for another goal in the match with Roberto Di Matteo running clear who had the chance to provide Hughes with a hat-trick. He expertly took it himself to ensure a 6-2 Chelsea victory, great game this one.

Three days later it was Southampton that visited Stamford Bridge which was a sell out. Another three points secured in a 1-0 win thanks to another fantastic goal from Gianfranco Zola. Chelsea were now up to fifth in the league but then came three league defeats in a row as we built up to the F.A Cup semi-final against Wimbledon. A 1-0 defeat at Middlesbrough before getting beaten 3-0 at home to Arsenal. Injuries and suspensions were apparent and it was the same in a midweek loss at Coventry. A game that is remembered for Chelsea being forced to wear the Coventry away kit by the referee due to a kit clash! Chelsea's chances of qualifying for the UEFA Cup via the league took a massive blow. Focus now turned back to the F.A Cup.

F.A Cup Semi-final
Date: Sunday 13th April 1997
Result: Wimbledon 0-3 Chelsea
Chelsea Goal Scorers:
Hughes (43, 90) Zola (64)
Venue: Highbury
Attendance: 32,674
Chelsea Team:
Grodas, Clarke, Johnsen, Leboeuf, Sinclair, Burley, Di Matteo, Newton, Wise, Hughes, Zola

What a truly fantastic day! Wimbledon were certainly another one of those teams that could cause an upset and it was obvious the crazy gang were going to try and do anything they could on and off the pitch to unsettle us. The game was played at Arsenal's Highbury Stadium with

Chelsea fans filling three sides of the ground. Chelsea were wearing the yellow 'ice cream' kit which was always a great sight.

The game was very even in the early stages but it was Mark Hughes who opened the scoring from close range shortly before half-time. Midway through the second-half saw Gianfranco Zola score one of his best goals in a Chelsea shirt. A pass from Di Matteo saw Zola turn backwards leaving defender Blackwell for dust before for curling the ball into the bottom corner. Chelsea fans were ecstatic behind the goal. Mark Hughes finished the game off in the last minute by riffling the ball into the top corner with his left foot. The usually so 'cool' Ruud Gullit jumped for joy as did the rest of the bench. The referee's whistle was blown and Chelsea were in the F.A Cup Final. That feeling was just fantastic, we would face Middlesbrough on May 17th at Wembley.

Going into the last five league games of the season it was impossible to not think of anything other than the F.A Cup Final. Players were understandably being rested despite Chelsea needing to finish in at least fifth position to qualify for the UEFA Cup. A 3-1 defeat at Newcastle was followed by a 2-1 win at home to Leicester. Chelsea would then face Wimbledon again, this time at Selhurst Park with Dan Petrescu scoring the only goal of the game. The final home game of the season saw Chelsea and Leeds play out a 0-0 draw before finishing the league season with a 2-1 win at Everton with Wise and Di Matteo getting the goals. It was a sixth place finish for Chelsea, our highest since 1990. It wasn't enough for a UEFA Cup spot but we still had the F.A Cup as a route into the European Cup Winners Cup.

The build-up to the F.A Cup Final was so exciting, I was fourteen at the time and the thought of Dennis Wise going up the famous Wembley steps gave me goose bumps. That thought along with the traditional F.A Cup song with Suggs, Blue Day was enough to get any Chelsea fan buzzing with excitement. I remember collecting all the football (Shoot and Match) magazines as we edged closer to the final and putting the posters up on my wall. I had also compiled a scrap book of Chelsea's cup run so far, the Evening Standard newspaper were also doing their bit providing Chelsea cup final posters. Middlesbrough were our opponents who had already lost the League Cup Final to Leicester and had been relegated from the Premier League the week before. They still had players that could hurt us but Chelsea went into the final as clear favourites to win the cup.

Two days before the cup final I remember me and my brother Steve discussing where we would watch it as it was never thought in a million years that we might get tickets and said we'd talk to dad when he got home from work. Soon after my dad walked through the front door we asked him what our plans were. He sat down and opened his briefcase and said, 'I was going to talk to you both about that tonight'. As he said it he pulled out three tickets for the final. We couldn't believe it and proceeded to jump up and down in the lounge. I knew even at fourteen he must have gone to some lengths to get tickets and he must have had to pay over the odds for them. Getting tickets for this match was virtually impossible.

The plan was to go to the game at Wembley and all being well we would go back to Fulham that night hopefully to celebrate and stay at my Nana's house who only lived round the corner from Stamford Bridge. On the day of the game there were certainly plenty of nerves but also so much excitement. Me and my dad proceeded to our local hairdressers where my dad had a quick haircut before the staff applied our face paints. Strange he had his hair cut in hindsight as he wore a Ruud Gullit wig all day! We met my dad's friends at a Pizza place in Victoria, my dad explained how he managed to get tickets, one of my dad's friends managed to get one in a box through work and the other two had tickets in the Middlesbrough end. My dad was so paranoid that someone would pinch our tickets he hid them in a polythene bag inside his sock! The atmosphere on the tube was brilliant with Chelsea fans signing throughout the journey which carried on up Wembley Way. There was a real sense that we were finally going to win a trophy! To my dad's relief we went through the turnstiles and before we got inside he placed a bet. We got to our seats around fifteen minutes before kick off and seeing that 'sea of blue' with flags and scarves stays in my mind.

F.A Cup Final
Date: Saturday 17th May 1997
Result: Chelsea 2-0 Middlesbrough
Chelsea Goal Scorers:
Di Matteo (1), Newton (83)
Venue: Wembley Stadium
Attendance: 79,160
Chelsea Team:
Grodas, Petrescu, Clarke, Leboeuf, Sinclair, Minto, Wise, Di Matteo, Newton, Hughes, Zola (Vialli 89)

The atmosphere in the ground throughout was amazing and the 'ten men went to mow' was perfectly timed as Middlesbrough kicked off. Dennis Wise almost immediately picked up a loose ball from the kick off and passed into the path of Roberto Di Matteo in our own half. He kept running with the ball and as Mark Hughes ran across, it opened up and Robbie shot from thirty yards with the ball coming off the underside of the crossbar and into the back of the net. Chelsea were 1-0 up after just 43 seconds! The celebrations were wild and to this day it is one of the most memorable goals I've ever witnessed which still gives me goose bumps when I see it now. It most certainly squashed some pre-match nerves.

We had to wait until the eighty-third minute to start feeling we were closing in on the cup. Eddie Newton started the move who passed to Dan Petrescu, a great cross to Gianfranco Zola whose clever back heel found the arriving Newton who scored from close range. A moment of pure ecstasy! There were a few nervy moments in the game but the F.A Cup was coming to Chelsea, our first major trophy for twenty-six years and something Matthew Harding would have been proud of, this was for him. Grown men and women in tears just couldn't quite believe we had done it with many dreams coming true 'When Wise went up to lift the F.A Cup, we were there, we were there'.

Shortly after vacating Wembley Stadium we headed back to Stamford Bridge where the celebrations carried on long into the night down the Fulham Road. I remember my dad's friend saying to me once we had all met up again, 'Never forget this moment Chris, you may never see Chelsea win anything again, me and your dad have had to wait a long time for this'. One of those conversations you have with an adult as a kid that you just don't forget. We stayed at my Nana's that night who lived locally and I remember how pleased she was that we'd won the cup. Lying on a camp bed trying to get some sleep I just couldn't, the buzz was incredible.

The next morning despite a short sleep I was still buzzing. Me and my brother Steve walked round to the local corner shop and bought a copy of every single Sunday newspaper. We had some breakfast, got ready and made the short walk back to the Fulham Road for the open top bus parade. Some fans had clearly not gone home and partied all night! The parade was great and this time it was even better with a trophy being passed around on the top deck. A 'Blue Day'? A magical blue weekend. Oh yea and the bet my dad had before the game? He put it on Roberto Di Matteo to score the first goal.

Summary of the 1996 - 97 season

Ruud Gullit and the team secured the club's first piece of major silverware since 1971! Winning the F.A Cup was truly magical with some fantastic wins on route to Wembley. The semi-final and the final were great but so was the comeback in the fourth round at home to Liverpool, we also have Erland Johnsen to thank for the Leicester game! The cup success was a great tribute to Matthew Harding who tragically lost his life in the October.

A sixth place finish was also a significant improvement and our highest placed finish since the 1989/90 season. Not that we'd sacrifice our cup success but we most probably would have finished higher if it wasn't for that.

The best league result and performance had to be the 2-1 victory at Old Trafford in the November.

Roberto Di Matteo had the most number of appearances with thirty-four and Mark Hughes finished as Chelsea's highest goal scorer with fourteen. Sparky was also crowned Chelsea player of the year, and rightly so. All of our new signings made a huge impact on the team and it is quite remarkable how well they all gelled together so quickly. A special mention to captain Dennis Wise, despite the arrival of so many fantastic players he remained the heartbeat of the team and the leader.

F.A Cup success meant Chelsea had qualified for the European Cup Winners Cup for the next season. Exciting times ahead.

1997 - 1998

Another very eventful summer at Stamford Bridge saw Jakob Kjeldbjerg, Terry Phelan, Erland Johnsen, Scott Minto, Paul Parker and Craig Burley leave the club. In came Dutch goalkeeper Ed De Goey, Bernard Lambourde, Celestine Babayaro, Gustavo Poyet, Tore Andre Flo and former blue Graeme Le Saux.

Some real quality added to an already star-studded squad. If we really wanted to compete on the European stage top reinforcements were most definitely needed.

There continued to be great excitement and anticipation going into the new season and a time where my dad decided to buy season tickets. There was a group of ten of us who would usually go to a handful of games a season and between the group eight season tickets were bought with two rows of four next to each other. With my brother Steve now at university I knew there would be an opportunity for me to attend many games. Excited? I was absolutely buzzing, Gate 15, MHL would be our home. The new Shed End was unveiled at the first home game but we always knew we'd want to be in the Matthew Harding Lower.

Most notably from the pre-season games was Chelsea winning the Umbro International Tournament for a consecutive year, this time at Goodison Park defeating Newcastle and Everton. There was also a penalty shootout defeat in the Charity Shield to Manchester United at Wembley.

There was definitely a feeling that we could improve on our sixth place finish from last season and have a good run in Europe. The summer saw the opening of the new Chelsea megastore. A big difference from the little club shop, I literally wanted everything and the launch saw Dennis Wise and Gianfranco Zola holding the F.A Cup on a scooter wearing the new 'Autoglass' kit. This also coincided with the redeveloped site being announced to the world as 'Chelsea Village' with its new hotels, bars and restaurants bringing an up-market flavour to the traditional stadium façade that had been Stamford Bridge of old.

The start of Chelsea's European Cup Winner's Cup campaign coincided with the launch of new television station Channel 5 and they would be showing our games.

We played our first three league games of the season away from Stamford Bridge as the finishing touches were being made to the new Shed End. First up was Coventry away in the August sunshine. Over 4,000 Chelsea fans made the trip to the Midlands but the game ended in defeat as Chelsea lost 3-2 late on. Next up was newly promoted Barnsley at Oakwell.

Premier League
Date: Sunday 24th August 1997
Result: Barnsley 0-6 Chelsea
Chelsea Goal Scorers:
Petrescu (25), Poyet (38), Vialli (44, 57, 65, 82)
Venue: Oakwell
Attendance: 18,170
Chelsea Team:
De Goey, Clarke, Myers, Sinclair, Petrescu (Granville 72), Le Saux, Di Matteo, Poyet (Nicholls 70), Wise, Vialli, Zola (Flo 55)

As any season starts many are still on their summer holidays, that was the case for me being away in Jersey with the family. A sunny afternoon saw us take to the beach, I said to my Dad shall we find somewhere to watch the game later. He was more than happy to find a pub along the sea front. We found a bar around half an hour before kick off and to our surprise it was full of Barnsley supporters. Feeling quite relaxed we were happy to just watch the game and we managed to get a table.

In a game that was completely one sided, Dan Petrescu opened the scoring with a clever shot in off the post and Gustavo Poyet soon made it

2-0 following up his initial saved header. Just before half-time it was 3-0, a long throw by Ed De Goey found Dan Petrescu, he played a great ball to Gianluca Vialli who spectacularly struck the ball on the half volley.

Shortly into the second-half Vialli scored a follow up header to his initial shot to make it 4-0 and later got his hat-trick from close range after Dennis Wise played him in. Goal number six came eight minutes from time and it was Vialli with his fourth on the half volley. A great result and performance, the bar started to empty more and more as the goals went in with me and my dad grinning from ear to ear.

A 2-0 win at Selhurst Park against Wimbledon followed with another welcomed clean sheet. Next up was our first home game of the season and the unveiling of the new Shed End. The West Stand was still a building site but was still able to accommodate a few supporters with no roof.

Premier League
Date: Saturday 30th August 1997
Result: Chelsea 4-2 Southampton
Chelsea Goal Scorers:
Petrescu (7), Leboeuf (28), Hughes (31), Wise (34)
Southampton Goal Scorers:
Davies (25), Monkou (59)
Venue: Stamford Bridge
Attendance: 28,832
Chelsea Team:
De Goey, Duberry, Leboeuf, Sinclair, Petrescu (Clarke 78), Le Saux, Di Matteo (Nicholls 71), Poyet, Wise, Hughes, Zola (Vialli 71)

It took Dan Petrescu just seven minutes to score the first goal at the new Shed End, and what a goal it was. A fantastic chip from outside the box which floated beautifully and went in off the post. The celebration involved the players polishing his boot. It didn't take long for Southampton to equalise and a moment to forget for goal keeper Ed De

Goey as he was caught in possession.

The lead was quickly restored by a brave Frank Leboeuf header and Mark Hughes soon made it 3-1 with a header of his own after a great cross from Graeme Le Saux. It was 4-1 before half-time as Dennis Wise tapped in after good work from Zola and Petrescu.

The second-half saw one more goal and it was former Chelsea favourite Ken Monkou who got it with Frank Sinclair seeing red later in the game. The match was already over and Chelsea ran out comfortable winners, there was a real buzz around Stamford Bridge and this was our first game as season ticket holders.

Another trip to Selhurst Park saw Chelsea win 3-0 but this time against Crystal Palace. Some great goals in this one and especially pleasing to see Graeme Le Saux on the score sheet for the first time since returning to the club.

Our first round, first leg game in the European Cup Winners Cup saw us face Slovan Bratislava at Stamford Bridge. A 2-0 victory live on recently launched Channel 5 set us up nicely for the second leg. A difficult next two games saw The Blues only get one point against Arsenal and Manchester United after conceding late in both games. We were back to winning ways soon enough beating Newcastle 1-0 at The Bridge and then winning 2-0 in Bratislava (thanks to Luca Vialli's backside).

A disappointing 4-2 defeat at Liverpool saw us well beaten and we scraped past Blackburn Rovers in a penalty shoot out League Cup victory. A late Frank Leboeuf rocket ensured three points against Leicester shortly before the team braved the snow in Norway.

European Cup Winners Cup, Second Round, First Leg
Date: Thursday 23rd October 1997
Result: Tromso 3-2 Chelsea
Tromso Goal Scorers:
Nilsen (6), Fermann (19), Arst (86)

BLUE DAYS

Chelsea Goal Scorers:
Vialli (85, 90)
Venue: Alfheim Stadion, Tromso
Attendance: 6,438
Chelsea Team:
De Goey, Clarke, Leboeuf (Myers 87), Sinclair, Granville (Hughes 46), Babayaro, Di Matteo, Newton, Wise, Vialli, Zola

This game surely has to go down as one of the strangest games in Chelsea history! The snow was cleared prior to kick off with the pitch not looking too bad. The second-half however was a complete shambles. The game was stopped twice as ground staff had to come out and clear the snow off the pitch. Both teams were playing in a blizzard, you could be forgiven for thinking every game was like a blizzard if your Channel 5 signal was anything like mine.

Not surprising the Tromso ground staff were quick to it as they were 2-0 up at half-time with Chelsea not playing well at all. It was clear the game should have been abandoned with Ruud Gullit making his feelings very clear on the Chelsea bench. Gianluca Vialli scored a fantastic and vital away goal five minutes from the end but Tromso quickly restored their two goal lead. As we approached injury time Luca scored another great solo goal leaving defenders sliding on the ground. We were poor on the night but the game will always be remembered for the blizzard and two wonderful goals from Vialli.

European away games on a Thursday night and then playing back in the Premier League on the Sunday is always difficult and a 1-0 defeat at Bolton proved that. A 2-0 win at Aston Villa thanks to Hughes and Flo saw Chelsea up to fourth with a game in hand. Next was Tromso at Stamford Bridge in the Cup Winners Cup second leg. A very small travelling contingent from Norway were welcomed inside the ground with 'You only sing when it's snowing'. It was a very straight forward night as Chelsea won 7-1 with an aggregate 9-4 score. Chelsea would now face Real Betis over two legs later on in the season.

A 2-1 victory over West Ham at The Bridge thanks to a magical Zola free-kick was followed up by another 2-1 extra-time victory over Southampton in the League Cup. Things were looking very good so a 1-0 defeat at Blackburn was disappointing especially after having many chances to win the match. Our game in hand was finally played, It took two late penalties for us to overcome a very poor Everton side at The Bridge. It really didn't matter though as we were now third and only three points off the top. Three days later it would be another home game against Derby County.

Premier League
Date: Saturday 29th November 1997
Result: Chelsea 4-0 Derby
Chelsea Goal Scorers:
Hughes (35), Zola (12, 66, 77)
Venue: Stamford Bridge
Attendance: 34,554
Chelsea Team:
De Goey, Duberry, Leboeuf, Sinclair, Petrescu, Babayaro, Le Saux, Di Matteo, Wise, Hughes (Flo 79), Zola (Crittenden 86)

When you're a kid certain games just stick out, I don't just mean the big one's but random ones as well. This game is most certainly one of those for me. It was the first time in a while that me, my dad and my brother all went to a game together. Our new dining spot before a game (and sometimes after) was La Rueda Spanish Tapas Bar on the Kings Road. It was always lively in there with great food and plenty of drinks. A table for eight before a match became a regular thing.

On paper it wasn't necessarily going to be an easy game, Derby were up to sixth and playing some impressive football themselves. Chelsea however ran riot, a great win with Gianfranco Zola scoring his first ever career hat-trick. The build-up play and finishing was top drawer and at this point in the season it was probably the best complete performance.

Next up was Spurs away, surely it couldn't be topped, could it?

Premier League
Date: Saturday 6th December 1997
Result: Tottenham Hotspur 1-6 Chelsea
Tottenham Goal Scorer:
Vega (43)
Chelsea Goal Scorers:
Flo (40, 63, 90), Di Matteo (48), Petrescu (59), Nicholls (78)
Venue:
White Hart Lane
Attendance:
28,476
Chelsea Team:
De Goey, Duberry, Leboeuf, Sinclair, Petrescu, Babayaro (Nicholls 20), Le Saux, Di Matteo, Wise, Flo, Zola

Chelsea were flying! With the game not on television I arranged to go out with my school friend to my local town centre for a bit of Christmas shopping. Walking around town in the afternoon I was desperate to find out how Chelsea were doing. I decided to pop into 'Dixons', as many of you will remember if you were out the best way to check football scores was always to go into an electrical shop and there would often be a gathering of football supporters around a T.V with Teletext on. I peered over and saw Chelsea were leading 2-1, absolutely buzzing and praying we could hold on despite it only being five minutes into the second-half.

Once I got home I instantly asked my dad what the final score was. He said, 'Chelsea won 6-1', with a big smile on his face. I said, 'Dad, don't mess about, what was the score?' He proceeded to put Teletext on and there it was, 6-1!!!!! I couldn't believe it! One of those nights where I stayed up to watch Match Of The Day so I knew it was true, instead of usually recording it on VHS and watching first thing in the morning. We were truly fantastic on the day with some great goals. Spurs just couldn't cope with Tore Andre Flo who scored a terrific hat-trick and Gianfranco Zola with four assists! Roberto Di Matteo, Dan Petrescu and Mark Nicholls were also amongst the goals in our biggest ever win at White Hart Lane.

The next match was frustrating with Leeds visiting The Bridge. They came with a game plan to wind us up and it worked, Leeds were reduced to nine men with some shocking fouls in the game. We couldn't find a way through and the game ended goalless. A great 4-1 win at Sheffield Wednesday had us thinking the Leeds game was just a blip, it wasn't. A 1-1 draw on Boxing Day at home to Wimbledon was frustrating. It got worse at Southampton losing 1-0, as a family we watched my brother Dan perform in an amateur dramatics play but I managed to listen to the game secretly on the radio with one headphone in. Sorry bruv.

After the festive period our attention turned to the F.A Cup. A packed Stamford Bridge saw the Manchester United fans in the uncovered West Stand. It was a big game and as holders the world's eyes were watching this third round tie in anticipation. It didn't go to plan and Chelsea were taught a serious lesson by a very good side. In a state of absolute shock Chelsea went 5-0 behind, Graeme Le Saux pulled one back with one of Chelsea's goals of the season which often gets forgotten due to the circumstances. Gianluca Vialli scored two to spare our blushes but many had left to go home by then. 5-3 doesn't sound too bad but we were definitely out played for the large majority of the game.

There was still another route back to Wembley for The Blues in the form of the League Cup. A quarter-final tie at Portman Road saw Ipswich Town take Chelsea to penalties after a 2-2 draw. Chelsea were victorious and would have to beat Arsenal over two legs to reach the final. It was at the next game at home to Coventry in which The Blues won 3-1 that we decided to get tickets for the first leg at Highbury. Before that game we suffered a disappointing 3-1 loss at Everton. After midweek fixtures Chelsea dropped down to fourth.

BLUE DAYS

League Cup Semi-final, First Leg
Date: Wednesday 28th January 1998
Result: Arsenal 2-1 Chelsea
Arsenal Goal Scorers:
Overmars (23), Hughes (47)
Chelsea Goal Scorer:
Hughes (68)
Venue: Highbury
Attendance: 38,114
Chelsea Team:
De Goey, Clarke, Duberry, Lambourde, Sinclair (Vialli 86), Petrescu (Charvet 46), Le Saux, Gullit, Newton, Flo (Hughes 59), Zola

Results had been indifferent of late and Arsenal were very much on course to win the title. It was always going to be difficult but our job was made harder as both Frank Leboeuf and Roberto Di Matteo were away playing international friendlies for their respective countries. Ruud Gullit himself played centre back and Laurent Charvet made his debut.

The Piccadilly Line train to Arsenal was lively with a large group of Chelsea fans in full voice. I can't say I was confident going into the game but I felt as long as we were still in the tie after ninety minutes we would certainly have a chance in the return leg at Stamford Bridge.

As we got in the ground we were right behind the goal with Chelsea fans packing out the whole clock end with an increased allocation of tickets as it was a cup match. To say Chelsea were loud prior to kick off would be an understatement.

The game itself was quite abysmal from Chelsea, we were completely outclassed for long periods and I remember feeling very nervous with every attack Arsenal had. We were 2-0 down shortly after half-time and if it wasn't for goalkeeper Ed De Goey it would have been so much worse.

Mark Hughes had been on the pitch less than ten minutes before scoring a vital away goal, which we most certainly didn't deserve. A deflected cross from Gianfranco Zola found Hughes to head past the outrushing goalkeeper, the scenes behind the goal were mental. A vital, vital away goal and we left the ground feeling we were still very much in the tie, amazing considering how poor we were. We'd go again in three weeks time.

With two defeats on the bounce we needed a straight forward win to restore confidence. That was exactly the case as we beat relegation threatened Barnsley 2-0 at home. It was then another trip to Arsenal, this time in the league before we faced them in the League Cup semi-final second leg. Another very poor performance, this time losing 2-0.

What happened next shocked the whole of World Football. Ruud Gullit was sensationally sacked on February 12th 1998. No one could understand it. Chelsea were sitting second in the Premier League, at the quarter-final stage of the Cup Winners Cup and in the League Cup semi-final. It was thought it was over contract negotiations, both camps had different opinions on what happened but it certainly left a sour taste in the mouth of us supporters. Chairman Ken Bates wasn't the easiest of people to get on with but it was a surprise how it all ended. I remember reading in the newspaper the next day a fan had gone down to the Harlington training ground and threw his Chelsea shirt in front of the players and walked off. There was however no time to dwell as we were at a pivotal stage of the season and Gianluca Vialli instantly replaced Ruud as our new player / manager.

League Cup Semi-final, Second Leg
Date: Wednesday 18th February 1998
Result: Chelsea 3-1 Arsenal
Chelsea Goal Scorers:
Hughes (10), Di Matteo (51), Petrescu (53)
Arsenal Goal Scorer:
Bergkamp (82 pen)
Venue: Stamford Bridge
Attendance: 34,330

Chelsea Team:
De Goey, Clarke, Duberry, Leboeuf, Petrescu, Le Saux, Di Matteo, Wise, Hughes, Vialli (Newton (80), Zola

So just six days after the sensational sacking of Gullit it would be Gianluca Vialli to lead the team against Arsenal in the League Cup semi-final, second leg at Stamford Bridge and a chance of reaching another final at Wembley. Throughout the whole era I speak about in this book this game is right up there with the best.

It was always going to be a big game but with the circumstances we were now in, it was even bigger. I remember the journey to the game and reading the sports section of the Evening Standard on the tube. No one gave us a chance after they beat us twice in recent weeks with ease.

In our usual MHL Gate 15 seats all the usual season ticket holders were there as it seemed everyone opted to get tickets for this one. The atmosphere was electric, just like it was at Highbury three weeks previously.

It was Mark Hughes who got the opening goal after just ten minutes with a clever shot on the turn to level things up on aggregate. Still very nerve racking but a perfect start.

Patrick Viera was sent off for a second yellow card after completely taking out Graeme Le Saux on the left wing. That certainly gave us an extra boost and we took full advantage of it as we quickly went 2-0 up. Vialli was down but the referee didn't think he was fouled, the ball eventually broke for Roberto Di Matteo who unleashed a rocket from thirty yards that riffled into the top corner. A magnificent goal at the Matthew Harding end and probably the best goal Robbie ever scored for Chelsea (okay maybe the 1997 F.A Cup Final).

The atmosphere was brilliant and things got even better just two minutes later. Arsenal failed to clear a corner and the ball fell to Dan Petrescu who dummied twice before coolly hitting the ball on the half volley into the bottom corner with Manninger once again having no chance. The scenes of celebration were wild by both players and fans.

Arsenal scored a penalty through Bergkamp with eight minutes remaining after Michael Duberry was alleged to have handled the ball. It was too little too late for Arsenal. Chelsea won 3-1 (4-3 on aggregate) and Gianluca Vialli had got Chelsea to Wembley after just one game in charge. It was later revealed Luca's team talk before the game consisted of a little drop of champagne. Very Chelsea that.

Clearly a hangover followed as we lost ground in the Premier League by losing 2-0 at Leicester and then 1-0 at home to Manchester United in a very early kick off.

It was then the return of the Cup Winners Cup with Chelsea playing Real Betis away in the first leg.

European Cup Winners Cup, Quarter-final, First Leg
Date: Thursday 5th March 1998
Result: Real Betis 1-2 Chelsea
Real Betis Goal Scorer:
Alfonso (46)
Chelsea Goal Scorer:
Flo (7, 12)
Venue: Benito Villamarin
Attendance: 31,000
Chelsea Team:
De Goey, Clarke, Duberry, Leboeuf, Sinclair, Petrescu, Di Matteo, Newton, Wise, Flo (Hughes 84), Zola (Nicholls 79)

As a kid I would always buy the season reviews on VHS and liked looking back at how crazy the Chelsea fans were going for particular goals, especially away from home. This was most definitely one of those matches.

Another Channel 5 night for me with the usual very excitable commentary from Johnathan Pearce. Chelsea were fantastic on the night and two goals in the first twelve minutes from Tore Andre Flo were expertly taken and very much set us on our way. There were many

Chelsea fans at the game who celebrated deliriously in the corner.

Betis got a goal back just after half-time but Chelsea held on and secured a great win. It was back to The Bridge in two weeks for the second leg with much belief that we could go on and win the competition.

Our league form was really starting to slip and we were becoming known as a cup team. Either side of a 6-2 win against Crystal Palace there were disappointing defeats at home to Aston Villa and away to West Ham. It was now time to focus on two cup competitions we very much had a chance of winning.

European Cup Winners Cup Quarter-final, Second Leg
Date: Thursday 19th March 1998
Result: Chelsea 3-1 Real Betis
Chelsea Goal Scorers:
Sinclair (30), Di Matteo (50), Zola (90)
Real Betis Goal Scorer:
George (21)
Venue: Stamford Bridge
Attendance: 32,300
Chelsea Team:
De Goey, Clarke, Duberry, Leboeuf, Sinclair, Petrescu (Lambourde 88), Di Matteo, Newton, Wise, Vialli, Zola

This was another great European night under the lights at Stamford Bridge. Despite having our two away goals I remember still feeling very nervous going into the match.

It didn't start well for us with Finidi George putting Betis ahead, Frank Sinclair headed us level to ease some nerves and that's how it stayed until half-time. Roberto Di Matteo scored five minutes into the second-half after a great solo run and finish which had us all thinking we were in the semi's. The icing on the cake came in the final minute with Gianfranco Zola scoring a fine effort from outside the box.

After the game we had some drinks to celebrate in the Shed Bar and when we came out we were fortunate to bump into both Jody Morris and Gianfranco Zola. A time before selfies it was an autograph on the back of my programme. My dad however didn't leave it there, he proceeded to give Gianfranco Zola a big kiss on his cheek. A great night, Chelsea would now face Italian side Vicenza over two legs in the semi-final.

Still sharing a season ticket with my older brother Steve, he decided he'd come back from university for the League Cup Final at Wembley. I couldn't complain as I had been to many more games than him during the season. It would be TV for me at a friends house.

Just like the season before Chelsea were favourites to beat Middlesbrough, a win would also secure European qualification for the next season.

League Cup Final
Date: Sunday 29th March 1998
Result: Chelsea 2-0 Middlesbrough (AET)
Chelsea Goal Scorers:
Sinclair (95), Di Matteo (107),
Venue: Wembley Stadium
Attendance: 77,698
Chelsea Team:
De Goey, Duberry, Leboeuf, Sinclair, Petrescu (Clarke 75), Le Saux, Di Matteo, Newton, Wise, Hughes (Flo 83), Zola

Chelsea dominated the game but found it desperately difficult to find a breakthrough. A frustrating match saw the game go into extra-time at 0-0 but just four minutes into it Chelsea finally broke the deadlock. Frank Sinclair burst forward and laid the ball off to Dennis Wise, it looked as if the ball would go out of play after a miscontrolled first touch, however Dennis managed to whip in a cross right on the by-line and right on to the head of Sinclair. A huge sigh of relief.

Roberto Di Matteo ensured the League Cup would be coming to

Chelsea as he sealed the game two minutes into the second period. Side footing home from a Zola corner after a Middlesbrough player slipped, another cup final goal Robbie could add to the growing collection.

A first trophy for player / manager Gianluca Vialli after being in the hot seat for just six weeks.

Just a few days after Chelsea's League Cup success at Wembley the players were flying out to Italy where we faced Vicenza in the Cup Winners Cup semi-final, first leg. Another competition we had a very good chance of winning, however we suffered a 1-0 defeat with it all to do at Stamford Bridge in the return.

Back to the Premier League saw us win 1-0 at Derby thanks to Mark Hughes but a disappointing 3-1 defeat at Leeds followed. Before our big European semi-final there was enough time to squeeze in a routine win against Spurs thanks to Vialli and Flo.

European Cup Winners Cup Semi-final, Second Leg
Date: Thursday 16th April 1998
Result: Chelsea 3-1 Vicenza
Chelsea Goal Scorers:
Poyet (35), Zola (51), Hughes (76)
Vicenza Goal Scorer:
Luiso (32)
Venue: Stamford Bridge
Attendance: 33,810
Chelsea Team:
De Goey, Clarke, Leboeuf, Duberry, Le Saux, Morris (Hughes 70), Newton (Charvet 70), Poyet, Wise, Vialli, Zola (Myers 81)

The second leg to this day still goes down as one of my favourite ever games at The Bridge. Going 1-0 down shortly after the half hour mark, many thought we were down and out and you couldn't really blame them. We needed three goals and we did exactly that. A clever rebound from Gustavo Poyet made it 1-1 going into half-time, even then I remember thinking we had a mountain to climb.

A bullet header from Gianfranco Zola after a great Vialli cross made it 2-1 shortly after half-time. The atmosphere was electric and there was now a feeling that we could do it! Six minutes after coming on as a substitute a wonderful Mark Hughes volley sent Stamford Bridge into a frenzy, a truly magnificent individual goal. What a game, what a night, we were in the final!

This game will remain as one of the best European nights at The Bridge despite it not being in Europe's top competition. Next stop Stockholm, where Chelsea would meet Stuttgart in the final.

Despite our cup success and a European final to come we now had three home league games on the bounce. A huge match against Liverpool was sandwiched between a 1-0 win against Sheffield Wednesday and a 1-0 defeat to Blackburn.

Premier League
Date: Saturday 25th April 1998
Result: Chelsea 4-1 Liverpool
Chelsea Goal Scorers:
Hughes (11, 78), Clarke (67), Flo (72)
Liverpool Goal Scorer:
Riedle (45)
Venue: Stamford Bridge
Attendance: 34,639
Chelsea Team:
Kharine, Clarke, Duberry, Leboeuf, Petrescu (Charvet 76), Le Saux, Di Matteo, Newton, Poyet, Hughes (Nicholls 81), Zola (Flo 30)

As the season was gradually coming to a close the club's main focus was Stockholm, that was most certainly the talk on the terraces with many fans planning on making the trip.

A trademark Mark Hughes header put us into an early lead after a great Graeme Le Saux cross. It looked like it would stay that way until half-time only for us to concede after Dmitri Kharine failed to hold on to an initial shot.

A rare goal for Steve Clarke put us in the lead midway through the second-half and five minutes later another assist from Le Saux found Tore Andre Flo who finished very well. The points were sealed by Hughes this time scoring a spectacular over head kick. A big win and a great performance.

A defeat away to Newcastle followed before we faced relegation threatened Bolton Wanderers on the final league game of the season. Chelsea won the match 2-0 but for long periods many inside Stamford Bridge were urging Bolton to score so they would stay up at the expense of Everton. Gianluca Vialli and Jody Morris got the goals that condemned Bolton to the First Division and it was a fourth place finish for Chelsea. This was the club's highest league finish since 1970! All eyes were now fully focused on Stuttgart in the European Cup Winners Cup Final.

Having recently turned fifteen and with school swimming trials the following day and amongst other reasons there was no chance I would be making it to Stockholm. However my dad Rick and his friend Ron Roberts decided to make the trip and this is how Ron recalled it to me.

"It was a late decision to go to the final for 'two' lads either side of fifty. It was an overnight in Essex before a 5am taxi on the day of the game to Stansted airport. We were travelling back that night so we packed very light and it was a dark and gloomy morning. The weather didn't improve by the time we got to the airport which was already packed with Chelsea. Rick had supplied us both with Union Jack boxer shorts to wear over our jeans, don't ask!

We checked in and went straight to the duty free shop for refreshments no beer or wine were left so it was two bottles of vodka mixing it with Kia-Ora, only juice available. The flight was already delayed, we then proceeded to get something to eat. A frantic game of football develops in the departure lounge, which consisted to big cheers as to who could kick it the highest. Amidst deafening boos police moved in to confiscate the ball, so probably they won! Mist / fog is lifting but the news is that our plane can't take off due to it being fog bound elsewhere. Rumour had it at this point that we were all going to be put on coaches to Gatwick for flights from there.

A couple of hours pass and Chelsea fans drinking Stansted airport dry our flight is finally called but amazingly there didn't seem to be a mad rush with many seem to be enjoying the Stansted experience. Once aboard it was amazing that they were serving drinks, it was the last thing we needed really! At last we landed in Stockholm but the plane keeps taxiing and eventually stops with the terminal building barely visible in the distance. Engines off, aircon off, doors remain closed. Fellow passengers are getting restless.

Finally we were allowed off and the reason for the delay is immediately obvious, a thick blue line to make sure we board the airport bendy bus, where else did they think we would go? Through the terminal and onto the package transport to town seems to take forever. No idea where we are dropped off but it didn't matter as all the bars were packed with Chelsea.

We're starving and it's past conventional lunch time. We find a place that is less busy. A decent meal and more drinks then we are joined by a big Swedish guy who insists that we need the local liqueur. Thick black stuff that tastes like Covonia going down. We stagger out looking for the tube station, it isn't too far, thank goodness! Does anyone know the ticketing policy? Nope, so over the barrier along with a small group of Chelsea fans in hope they know where they're going."

European Cup Winners Cup Final
Date: Saturday Wednesday 13th May 1998
Result: Chelsea 1-0 Stuttgart
Chelsea Goal Scorer:
Zola (71)
Venue: Rasunda Stadium, Stockholm, Sweden
Attendance: 30,216

Chelsea Team:
De Goey, Clarke, Duberry, Leboeuf, Granville, Petrescu, Di Matteo, Poyet (Newton 81), Wise, Flo (Zola 70), Vialli

Ron continues with his account of events. "Long queues at the stadium and with our late tickets we are in the lower stand at the Stuttgart end, a very colourful lot, lots of scarfs to every appendage. Fortunately they are in the upper tier and the whole lower tier is Chelsea meaning The Blues are very well represented on all four sides of the ground.

The teams are out, no Zola for us but he is on the bench. The first-half passes with a bit of a blur. Still feeling a little worse for wear Zola is now on and instantly scores on the half volley after a great ball from Dennis Wise. The stadium truly erupts. Back in town after the game many Chelsea fans turn out to carry on the celebrations. I know we ended up in another club but don't remember a great deal. The Swedish police were great throughout laughing and joking with us.

Negotiations for a taxi to the airport are not that straight forward as we don't have enough Krona but we find a guy who accepts part payment in sterling. The airport is busy but in complete confusion so we check-in and go through to departures which, strangely is virtually deserted. I lie down across several seats and fall asleep. Being of stronger stuff Rick focuses on finding a flight home and I'm awoken by the news that we have a flight if we go NOW! No ticket needed, a glance at the passports but nothing noted and we are ushered on board before the pilot loses the take off slot. Looking around there is no more than twenty of us on the plane but he's moving as the doors are shut. We seek reassurance that this plane is going to Stansted. Mid flight it occurs to me that if this plane is lost in the North Sea nobody will know what happened to us! A fantastic trip with a not so good hangover. We were back home in under twenty-four hours and Chelsea had won a European Trophy."

While my dad and Ron were traipsing around Stockholm me and my brother Steve watched it at home. So very nervous but it ended in pure ecstasy jumping around the lounge like lunatics when Zola volleyed into the top corner. A truly wonderful end to the season.

Summary of the 1997 - 98 season

Like many this season holds a special place with some fantastic memories. When Ruud was sacked in the February it left supporters in complete shock but with no time to dwell. At such a pivotal stage of the season Gianluca Vialli stepped up and delivered both the League Cup and European Cup Winners Cup. We played some great scintillating football at times although defensive improvements were needed.

Top goal scorer for the season was the man himself Vialli with nineteen in all competitions, most number of appearances was Frank Lebouef with forty-seven and player of the year deservedly went to captain Dennis Wise. Special mentions also have to go to Gustavo Poyet, Tore Andre Flo, Gianfranco Zola and Mark Hughes.

Emphatic league wins at Barnsley and Spurs scoring six goals showed we could most certainly blow teams away. Consistency in the league again hindered any chance of a title challenge but that was always going to happen with being involved and progressing in cup competitions.

Memorable trips to Tromso, Betis and Vicenza showed what we had to overcome to win our first European trophy since 1971.

Other games that stood out at Stamford Bridge included the return leg against Real Betis and Vicenza, league wins against Derby, Crystal Palace and Liverpool and not forgetting The League Cup semi-final win over Arsenal.

1998 - 1999

After our cup success all eyes were now on Chelsea to see if we could make a serious title challenge. It was felt we weren't far away and with a few more quality additions we could most certainly have a chance.

Chelsea continued to spend and Gianluca Vialli was now starting to put his own stamp on the team. Fresh from winning the World Cup was Marcel Desailly who arrived from AC Milan, Spanish international full back Albert Ferrer signed from Barcelona, Danish international Brian Laudrup and record signing Italian international Pierluigi Casiraghi also joined the club. There was a fantastic international feel to the squad with Captain Dennis Wise in the centre of it.

Notable players that moved on were Danny Granville, Mark Hughes and long term players Frank Sinclair and Steve Clarke.

There was nothing of real significance in pre-season as it was just five weeks after the World Cup Final that the new season began. With many of our players involved in the competitions' later stages, preparations were always going to be difficult.

For a second season running it was a trip to Highfield Road for the opening game of the season. A 2-1 defeat wasn't an ideal start with high expectations despite playing well and creating a lot of chances. A 1-1 draw followed at home to Newcastle before the team headed to Monaco.

European Super Cup Final
Date: Friday 28th August 1998
Result: Chelsea 1-0 Real Madrid
Chelsea Goal Scorer:
Poyet (81)
Venue: Stade Louis II Monaco
Attendance: 11,589

Chelsea Team:
De Goey, Ferrer, Desailly, Duberry, Leboeuf, Babayaro, Le Saux, Di Matteo (Poyet 63), Wise, Casiraghi (Flo 90), Zola (Laudrup 83)

Some may see the Super Cup as a glorified friendly but it was most certainly a big deal for us. A chance of a European trophy we had never won before and also to test our squad against one of the best teams in the world.

It was always going to be a hard game against Real Madrid and many didn't give us a chance against the Champions League winners. A late Gustavo Poyet strike beautifully placed into the bottom corner was enough to win the Super Cup. You could tell what it meant to the players as they celebrated afterwards. It was so important to keep that winning mentality as Chelsea won their fourth trophy in sixteen months.

With the first piece of silverware in the trophy cabinet Chelsea were still looking for a first league win. A frustrating 0-0 draw with Arsenal came before a 2-1 win against Nottingham Forest. A 1-0 home victory against Swedish cup winners Helsingborgs in the first leg of the first round of the Cup Winners Cup was shortly before a trip to Ewood Park.

Premier League
Date: Monday 21st September 1998
Result: Blackburn Rovers 3-4 Chelsea
Blackburn Goal Scorers:
Sutton (22, 79 pen), Perez (57)
Chelsea Goal Scorers:
Zola (15), Leboeuf (51 pen), Flo (82, 86)
Venue: Ewood Park
Attendance: 23,113
Chelsea Team:
De Goey, Ferrer, Desailly, Duberry, Leboeuf, Babayaro, Le Saux, Poyet, Wise (Di Matteo 54), Casiraghi (Flo 78), Zola (Laudrup 70)

This was an incredible game and probably one of Chelsea's most exciting in the Premier League era. I remember my brother going to our local pub to watch this one as I was gutted I couldn't see it. A school night and still no Sky in my household meant I had to listen to the game on the radio.

It was a fiery encounter with lots of chances for both teams. After Casiraghi was fouled outside the box it gave us a great chance to take the lead from a free-kick. Blackburn knew what was coming but couldn't do anything to stop it. An exquisite free-kick from Zola went up and over the wall and into the corner.

Zola had another one cleared off the line but soon after Chris Sutton equalised from close range as Chelsea failed to clear.

Shortly after half-time Zola was brought down in the area by goalkeeper Tim Flowers after a clever 1-2. It was debatable but a penalty was given with Frank Leboeuf converting. Chelsea in the lead, Roy Hodgson was furious.

Six minutes later the game was level after a mistake from De Goey left Perez free to tap-into an empty net. Perez got booked for a nasty tackle on Le Saux and there was clearly some tension between the two of them. It wasn't long before they were both again caught up in an altercation. Le Saux retaliated and struck Perez with his arm and as a result they were both sent off.

Blackburn were awarded a penalty after a foul by Duberry with Sutton converting, I remember having that sinking feeling that it wasn't going to be our night.

Tore Andre Flo and Brian Laudrup were brought on in the later stages of the game. Laudrup produced a fantastic cross after receiving the ball back and found the arriving Flo who volleyed in. Chelsea were back level and there was now a feeling that a draw was a good result in a very jam-packed game.

However, Flo wasn't finished yet! Just four minutes later the unthinkable happened. A long ball forward found Flo who beat the offside trap. The pass was on to Laudrup who was available unmarked. Flo went alone and slotted home as he fell to the ground from incoming challenges and ball nestled into the bottom corner. A great win as I proceeded to jump around my lounge! I remember being woken up that night by my brother as he returned from the pub singing Chelsea songs.

The next day I was back at school and during a P.E. lesson I managed to break my wrist whilst falling awkwardly playing basketball. With mum and dad both at work my brother Steve was called who walked round to the school. As I sat in the ambulance with him in complete agony I wondered who was feeling worse.

A 2-0 victory at home to Middlesbrough and progression to the next round of the Cup Winners Cup set us up to face Liverpool at Anfield in the league. A game that saw Casiraghi score his first Chelsea goal (I hope Phil Babb has recovered) in a 1-1 draw. We were unlucky not to win the match and played very well. A 2-1 win against Charlton and a 0-0 draw at Leeds were played either side of a 1-1 draw at home to Copenhagen in the Cup Winners Cup. The League Cup which was now known as the Worthington Cup saw Chelsea play Aston Villa at The Bridge as we started our defence. An emphatic 4-1 victory was remembered for a Vialli hat-trick and a certain youth player making his debut, his name was John Terry. Chelsea would now face Arsenal at Highbury in the next round.

The return leg in the Cup Winners Cup saw Chelsea win 1-0 away and progress to the next round. The talk before the game was all about 'homesick' Brian Laudrup and how it was likely he would return to his native Denmark. In the most bizarre of circumstances it would be Laudrup that scored the only goal of the match to knock the team out who he was to sign for the next day. The next week Chelsea were back in talks with Copenhagen where we arranged a deal for the highly rated Bjarne Goldbaek. Chelsea now went to Upton Park fourteen games unbeaten in all competitions.

Premier League

Date: Sunday 8th November 1998

Result: West Ham United 1-1 Chelsea

West Ham Goal Scorer:

Ruddock (4)

Chelsea Goal Scorer:

Babayaro (76)

Venue: Upton Park

Attendance: 26,023

Chelsea Team:

De Goey, Ferrer, Desailly, Lambourde, Babayaro, Le Saux, Di Matteo (Petrescu 46), Poyet, Wise, Casiraghi (Flo 24), Zola (Nicholls 66)

Two of my school friends had season tickets at West Ham in the Bobby Moore Upper Tier and one of them couldn't go to this match. The ticket was offered to me on the day for just £15, I couldn't say no! To be fair I didn't hesitate. Growing up in Essex most of my friends at school were West Ham fans or for some strange reason Manchester United. On a couple of occasions I joined them in the school holidays going down to the Chadwell Heath training ground. Looking back now the highlights were meeting Frank Lampard and Joe Cole! Having no idea at the time how good they would be for Chelsea.

Predictably before the game my dad said what every dad would, 'you're gonna have to keep your mouth shut!' I get he was a little worried but I was just buzzing I had a ticket. When we got inside Upton Park I instantly looked over at the packed Chelsea fans and could hear echo's of Carefree.

It didn't start well for us as we went behind to a Neil Ruddock free-kick after just four minutes. It was the day where Pierluigi Casiraghi's playing career came to an end. A horrible collision with West Ham goalkeeper Shaka Hislop left Casiraghi in agony just in front of the Chelsea fans. I was sat at the opposite end of the ground and we all knew instantly it didn't look good.

This Chelsea team had so much character and never knew when it was beaten and this was the type of fixture we would probably lose in previous seasons. A point was salvaged late on from a Celestine Babayaro header that sent the Chelsea fans wild behind the goal. I had to just sit there and do my best not to burst but on the inside I was screaming. In all honesty I was more than happy with a point, especially coming from behind. The banter at school the next day would have been tough had we not equalised.

League Cup Fourth Round
Date: Wednesday 11th November 1998
Result: Arsenal 0-5 Chelsea
Chelsea Goal Scorers:
Leboeuf (34 pen), Vialli (49, 73), Poyet (65, 80)
Venue: Highbury
Attendance: 37,562
Chelsea Team:
Kharine, Duberry, Leboeuf (Lambourde 82), Petrescu, Babayaro, Di Matteo, Goldbaek (Percassi 77), Poyet, Flo, Nicholls (Clement 77), Vialli

Just three days later it was another London derby and this time it was Arsenal at Highbury in the League Cup. My dad went to this one as a bit of a 'boys night' so none of us kids were there. I decided to watch it at a a school friend's house, the same friend I went to the West Ham game with. He had Sky and I didn't. I remember feeling very nervous before the match as the game at Highbury the season before in the same cup was very tough.

Shortly before the game much talk was about the line-ups and more focus was on the Arsenal team rather than ours in relation to the changes Wenger had made. It must be said though that the Arsenal eleven still cost significantly more than the team Vialli put out.

Once again Chelsea had the whole Clock End, every seat sold. Wow, Wow, Wow, Wow! What a game, what a Chelsea performance!

Frank Leboeuf got us off to the perfect start from the penalty spot after Poyet had been brought down. That certainly steadied the initial nerves as Kharine had to make some good saves up to that point. Shortly after half-time it was 2-0, a great ball from Goldbaek found Vialli who was able to beat the goalkeeper to the ball and finish into an empty net.

Another great ball from Goldbaek found Flo on the wing, winning an initial challenge he crossed for Poyet to finish from close range. It was soon 4-0 with Vialli scoring on the half volley after a delicious side foot assist from Poyet. It would be Gus himself to finish the scoring after being fed through by Petrescu, a great night for Chelsea and into the Quarter-final.

1-2, 1-2-3, 1-2-3-4, 5-0!

Three days later it was back to Stamford Bridge and you could tell that fans were still buzzing from midweek. Playing Wimbledon but constantly hearing new songs which made reference to a certain Arsenal manager. A 3-0 win made the party atmosphere even better and a 4-2 win at Leicester the following week left us five points behind league leaders Aston Villa with a game in hand and with them to come to The Bridge. Things were going so well but Chelsea were to have a little wobble.

A shock defeat to Wimbledon in the League Cup was sandwiched between two league draws against Sheffield Wednesday and Everton.

Premier League
Date: Wednesday 9th December 1998
Result: Chelsea 2-1 Aston Villa
Chelsea Goal Scorers:
Zola (30), Flo (90)
Aston Villa Goal Scorer:
Hendrie (32)
Venue: Stamford Bridge
Attendance: 34,765

Chelsea Team:
De Goey, Ferrer, Duberry, Desailly, Leboeuf, Petrescu, Babayaro (Poyet 79), Le Saux, Di Matteo, Vialli, Zola (Flo 66)

A midweek fixture against high flying Aston Villa was never going to be easy. It was a game in hand due to our participation in the Super Cup Final in August.

Chelsea were great on the night and fully deserved victory, The Bridge was buzzing! Zola put us in the lead on the half hour mark with a trademark free-kick only for Lee Hendrie to equalise two minutes later.

Chelsea dominated the second-half and hit the woodwork twice through Leboeuf and Le Saux as Chelsea piled on the pressure. Villa manager John Gregory's salute to the away fans was premature. Three minutes into injury time Flo (who was now on for Zola) rose to score a header from Di Matteo's corner. The scenes around the ground were brilliant, a huge win.

A 2-2 draw at Derby was disappointing having controlled the game and conceding late. Poyet and Flo with the goals again showing their importance to the team. Next stop, Old Trafford.

Premier League
Date: Wednesday 16th December 1998
Result: Manchester United 1-1 Chelsea
Manchester United Goal Scorer:
Cole (45)
Chelsea Goal Scorer:
Zola (83)
Venue: Old Trafford
Attendance: 55,159
Chelsea Team:
De Goey, Ferrer, Duberry, Lambourde, Petrescu, Babayaro, Le Saux (Poyet 44), Di Matteo, Wise, Flo, Zola

Chelsea were having a tendency to play very well away at big clubs but not always come away with anything to show for it. That was starting to change under Vialli and an away midweek game just before Christmas at Old Trafford was a great example of that.

I remember the game well and being in my local pub with my dad, brother and a friend and although there were the usual pre-match nerves we knew we were more than capable of causing an upset.

We played so well on the night and were unfortunate to go 1-0 down right on half-time through Andy Cole. Chelsea stayed in the game throughout the second-half and finally got our deserved equaliser with seven minutes remaining. A fantastic little flick from Poyet allowed Zola to get through the United defence and chip the ball over the outrushing Peter Schmeichel. Wild celebrations all round with a few chairs getting knocked over in the pub and Dennis Wise celebrating with the team putting his finger to his lips to silence Old Trafford. Chelsea were the team that looked like they'd go on to win the game. A thirty yard screamer from Babayaro hit the outside of the post in the last minute. A point we were very proud of.

A 2-0 victory over Tottenham at Stamford Bridge a few days later thanks to late Poyet and Flo goals quickly followed. Chelsea went top of the league with the win and it was now twenty games undefeated against Tottenham. Boxing Day saw The Blues travel to the south coast.

Premier League
Date: Saturday 26th December 1998
Result: Southampton 0-2 Chelsea
Chelsea Goal Scorers:
Flo (20), Poyet (48)
Venue: The Dell
Attendance: 15,253
Chelsea Team:
De Goey, Ferrer, Duberry, Leboeuf, Petrescu, Babayaro, Goldbaek, Morris, Poyet (Terry 73), Flo (Nicholls 83), Zola

Exactly half way through the league season now and with Chelsea top every game was vital and a must win to continue our title pursuit.

Another solid performance and result at Southampton thanks to Flo and Poyet who were in great form, however it came at a cost. The win was over shadowed by a bad injury for Poyet. A poor challenge from Colleter left him being stretchered off with knee ligament damage and out for three months.

An evening game at home to Manchester United in between Christmas and New Year saw Chelsea drop points. We certainly had the best chances to win the game but a 0-0 draw meant Aston Villa returned to the top of the league. A routine F.A Cup third round tie at Oldham saw Vialli get both goals in a 2-0 victory. Our injury list increased though with Flo going off and leaving on crutches.

There was soon to be better news as Chelsea won 1-0 at Ruud Gullit's Newcastle thanks to a single goal from Petrescu. Albeit on goal difference Chelsea were back at the top.

Premier League
Date: Saturday 16th January 1999
Result: Chelsea 2-1 Coventry City
Chelsea Goal Scorers:
Leboeuf (45), Di Matteo (90)
Coventry Goal Scorer:
Huckerby (9)
Venue: Stamford Bridge
Attendance: 34,869
Chelsea Team:
De Goey, Ferrer (Goldbaek 85), Lambourde, Leboeuf, Petrescu, Babayaro, Le Saux, Di Matteo, Wise, Vialli, Zola

I have to admit I felt confident going into this one as form was good despite injury problems. So it was a bit of a shock as to how poorly we played, it was like the players had never met each other before.

Coventry were in a relegation fight and we struggled to break them down. It was them that unexpectedly took the lead through Huckerby and were unfortunate not to increase their lead after hitting the woodwork. It would have to take something special for Chelsea to equalise and that's exactly what happened. An absolute belter right on half-time from Leboeuf saved our blushes.

The second-half was similar with Chelsea finding it very difficult to find any kind of rhythm. There was a huge touchline scuffle in injury time which delayed the game, it was going to be a late ending. I remember the Chelsea faithful making their feelings very clear to Coventry manager Gordon Strachan.

Again it was going to have to take something special to win the game and time was most definitely running out. Standing anxiously behind the goal in the MHL Stand, I watched Roberto Di Matteo hit an absolute stunner from outside the box which came off the underside of the cross bar and into the net. The scenes were fantastic with one fan crowd surfing near us. Chelsea remained top with no league defeat in twenty-one games. There was now a sense that Chelsea could quite possibly go on and win it.

Our form did not improve in the F.A Cup fourth round with it taking a last minute controversial penalty by Frank Leboeuf to save Chelsea from embarrassment at Oxford. We really were poor and things didn't get better as we went on to lose our second league game of the season going down 1-0 at Arsenal. The replay against Oxford in the F.A Cup was an unwanted fixture but a game we could look to rediscovering some form.

F.A Cup Fourth Round Replay
Date: Wednesday 3rd February 1999
Result: Chelsea 4-2 Oxford United
Chelsea Goal Scorers:
Wise (13), Zola (40), Forssell (46, 53)

Oxford Goal Scorers:
Gilchrist (5), Windass (77 pen)
Venue: Stamford Bridge
Attendance: 32,106
Chelsea Team:
De Goey, Petrescu, Desailly, Leboeuf (Terry 59), Babayaro, Le Saux, Di Matteo (Goldbaek 74), Morris, Wise, Forssell (Nicholls 66), Zola

It was an important win but was expected, however it was vital to rediscover some form. This game will always be remembered for a Stamford Bridge debut for seventeen year old Mikael Forssell.

Oxford took an unexpected 1-0 lead early on, a bizarre goal that came off Marcel Desailly. It didn't take long for a Chelsea equaliser with Wise finishing well from Zola's assist. Five minutes before half-time Chelsea took the lead after a superb chip from Zola just outside the box.

Straight after the break Mikael Forssell curled one beautifully into the top corner to everyone's surprise. His great home debut didn't end there as he scored another, this time a belter from outside the box after being laid off by Babayaro.

The only down side to the night was Dennis Wise being sent off late on. Trying to recover from his initial error Dennis blocked a shot with his hand. Oxford scored from the resulting penalty but it wasn't enough and Chelsea would face Sheffield Wednesday at Hillsborough in the fifth round.

Still missing Poyet and Flo Chelsea scraped a 1-0 win at home to Southampton thanks to a trademark Zola free-kick and Chelsea progressed to the F.A Cup quarter-final stage after winning 1-0 at Sheffield Wednesday thanks to a late Di Matteo goal. Relegation threatened Blackburn equalised late on at Stamford Bridge in a frustrating 1-1 draw which resulted in Vialli seeing red and Leboeuf missing a penalty. A 3-1 win at Nottingham Forest was pleasing and a return for Tore Andre Flo was an added bonus. Chelsea were still very much in the title race with Liverpool to come next.

Premier League
Date: Saturday 27th February 1999
Result: Chelsea 2-1 Liverpool
Chelsea Goal Scorers:
Leboeuf (7 pen), Goldbaek (38)
Liverpool Goal Scorer:
Owen (77)
Venue: Stamford Bridge
Attendance: 34,822
Chelsea Team:
De Goey, Ferrer, Desailly, Leboeuf (Lambourde 33), Petrescu, Le Saux (Newton 82), Di Matteo, Goldbaek, Morris, Flo (Forssell 86), Zola

This was a much better performance, reminiscent of earlier season form. We got off to the perfect start and it was Leboeuf scoring from the penalty spot after a handball from Phil Babb. A 2-0 cushion at half-time was thanks to Goldbaek after good play that involved both Petrescu and Zola.

Graeme Le Saux and Robbie Fowler were at each other for most of the game. Fowler was initially booked for a foul on Le Saux but Fowler continued to try and get a reaction and proceeded to stick his bum out. That delayed the taking of the free-kick and it was quite ridiculous that the referee proceeded to book Le Saux for time wasting. Le Saux most definitely got his revenge on Fowler in an 'off the ball' incident that wasn't picked up by the officials.

Michael Owen capitalised on a rare mistake from Desailly but Chelsea went on to win the game 2-1. A very good win and performance.

It was now the return of the cup competitions and before a trip to Old Trafford it was Valerenga in the ECWC. A straight forward first leg win was exactly what we needed with a 3-0 victory thanks to Babayaro, Zola and Wise.

F.A Cup Quarter-final

Date: Sunday 7th March 1999
Result: Manchester United 0-0 Chelsea
Venue: Old Trafford
Attendance: 54,587
Chelsea Team:
De Goey, Ferrer, Desailly, Lambourde, Petrescu (Newton 46), Le Saux, Di Matteo, Goldbaek, Morris, Flo (Forssell 60), Zola (Myers 80)

Apart from local-ish games and London derbies I view this match as my first proper away day. My brother was still at University in Staffordshire so he joined our train further down the line.

There were seven of us who met at London Euston to board our train to Manchester. It was an early start for us all as it was a 2pm kick off. From the minute I woke up on the day I was absolutely buzzing and it was great seeing so many Chelsea fans on the same train. To my surprise there were a few United fans on there as well.

The train journey felt like forever as it does when you're a kid but the buzz kept me going throughout. This was a time when I would soon be taking my GCSE's. I struggled academically, the school were kind enough to get me a Dictaphone so I could record lessons and refer back to things being taught in my own time. So naturally as soon as I got it I took it with me to Old Trafford to record Chelsea's away atmosphere.

When we got to Old Trafford it was a little different to how my dad and his friends remembered it having not been back since the 1970 F.A Cup Final replay! Around 7,000 Chelsea fans had made the trip and what an atmosphere it was!

Defensively Chelsea were solid on the day and we just did enough to earn the replay. Our best chance fell to Jody Morris whose shot was easily saved in the end after finding space. We certainly had to ride our luck at times and it didn't help playing over half the match with ten players. Two silly bookings for Roberto Di Matteo saw him sent off just before half-time.

Late in the second-half United went down to ten men also as Paul Scholes was dismissed. Chelsea fans were in full voice throughout the game and the players got a fantastic response when appreciating our support. A great day out with a replay to come just three days later.

The excitement of a replay against Manchester United was quickly gone as United took the lead after just two minutes. Chelsea pressured well and had chances but United killed the game in the second-half with Yorke scoring again. This was our first defeat at Stamford Bridge and things got worse in the league in our next game as West Ham won 1-0 to inflict our first home league defeat. Injuries and suspensions didn't help but this was a huge blow in the title race. A 3-2 win away to Valerenga saw our progression in the Cup Winners Cup however focus was very much still on the league with a big game against Aston Villa.

Premier League
Date: Sunday 21st March 1999
Result: Aston Villa 0-3 Chelsea
Chelsea Goal Scorers:
Flo (59, 90), Goldbaek (86)
Venue: Villa Park
Attendance: 39,217
Chelsea Team:
De Goey, Ferrer, Desailly, Leboeuf, Petrescu (Lambourde 79), Le Saux, Goldbaek, Morris, Wise, Flo (Nicholls 90), Zola

This was a huge game in the title race and a must win for Chelsea. Villa had dropped down the table but still had European qualification to play for.

Chelsea were superb on the day, playing some excellent football. Zola and Flo were denied in the first-half and we should have been in the lead at the break.

The breakthrough finally happened nearly an hour into the game. A fantastic pass from Ferrer put Flo through on the right hand side, fending off Gareth Southgate and quick feet allowed Flo to curl a low shot into the far corner.

Chelsea made it 2-0 four minutes from time with Goldbaek smashing home after a great ball from Flo right in front of the travelling Chelsea fans. The game was finished off in injury time with Flo scoring his second of the game after a neat pass from Jody Morris.

A great win that was fully deserved, Chelsea still very much in the title race and in the Cup Winners Cup.

A 1-0 win at The Valley thanks to Roberto Di Matteo kept us in and amongst it in the league and then we went on to draw 1-1 at Stamford Bridge against Real Mallorca in the Cup Winners Cup semi-final first leg. A win at Wimbledon and a draw followed away to Middlesbrough. Poyet was now back from his injury which he sustained on Boxing Day. Next was Leicester at home in the league which on paper looked a formality.

Premier League
Date: Sunday 18th April 1999
Result: Chelsea 2-2 Leicester City
Chelsea Goal Scorers:
Zola (30), Elliot (o.g 69)
Leicester Goal Scorer:
Duberry (o.g 82), Guppy (88)
Venue: Stamford Bridge
Attendance: 34,535
Chelsea Team:
De Goey, Ferrer (Duberry 74), Desailly, Leboeuf, Petrescu, Di Matteo, Goldbaek (Le Saux 46), Morris (Poyet 70), Wise, Flo, Zola

I remember going to this one with my brother as my dad couldn't make it. Despite the spirit Leicester had under Martin O'Neil it was certainly a game we were expected to win.

Chelsea dominated from the very start and went 1-0 up after half an hour with a fantastic lob from Gianfranco Zola. It was 2-0 with twenty minutes remaining after a lob from Petrescu came off the post and hit the unfortunate Elliot on the rebound. The atmosphere was great with a real buzz around the ground.

Eight minutes from time substitute Michael Duberry scored an own-goal as Leicester were on the attack. It was certainly a nervous ending and it really shouldn't have been as Chelsea were in control for much of the match. Two minutes from time Steve Guppy curled one from outside the box which De Goey couldn't get near. It was an awful feeling and two points thrown away at such a vital stage of the season. This was a real turning point for many fans that this game had killed any title hopes we had. Even now when I watch Chelsea and we're leading 2-0 I often think back to this match and am desperate for us to kill the game.

It was like the stuffing had really been knocked out of us after the Leicester game and confidence was low. Exit from the Cup Winners came next after losing 1-0 away in Mallorca (2-1 on aggregate) and a lacklustre 0-0 at Hillsborough followed. It was important that we didn't let this season fall apart as there were so many positives. Manchester United and Arsenal were battling it out for the Premier League but Chelsea's chances were very slim. Champions League qualification however was very much in our reach (the top three qualified back then).

A 3-1 home win against Everton installed confidence going into the Leeds game. They were fourth and trying to catch us, a win for Chelsea would secure Champions League football for the first time in our history.

Premier League
Date: Wednesday 5th May 1999
Result: Chelsea 1-0 Leeds United
Chelsea Goal Scorer:
Poyet (68)
Venue: Stamford Bridge
Attendance: 34,762

Chelsea Team:
De Goey, Ferrer, Desailly, Leboeuf, Petrescu, Le Saux, Morris (Goldbaek 66), Poyet, Wise, Flo (Di Matteo 82), Zola (Forssell 89)

This game will always stay in my memory, not only was it a huge match but it was also my 16th Birthday!

Stamford Bridge was absolutely buzzing on a great night under the lights. It was certainly a nervy one as it had so much resting on it. The breakthrough came midway through the second-half, a wonderful cross from Le Saux found the arriving Gustavo Poyet who headed past Nigel Martyn.

It was enough to win the game and Chelsea had qualified for the Champions League and finishing in the top three for only the fifth time in our history. We would have to overcome a qualifier but on the way home I remember buzzing with excitement with the thought of Chelsea playing against some of the best teams in Europe.

There were still two games to play in the league, a 2-2 draw at Tottenham with an absolute belter from Goldbaek and finishing the season with a home win over Derby. Vialli's playing days were over and he signed off by scoring the second goal.

Summary of the 1998 - 99 season

Our only silverware came early on in the season in the form of the Super Cup after a great win against European giants Real Madrid in Monaco. However there was much to be positive about, consistency in the league had Chelsea very much in the title race right up until the later stages of the season. Losing just three league games and finishing just four points behind eventual winners Manchester United.

The home defeat to West Ham in March and letting a two goal lead slip at home to Leicester in April were season defining for us.

A League Cup defeat to Wimbledon was disappointing considering our 5-0 win at Highbury in the previous round. The F.A Cup defeat to

BLUE DAYS

Manchester United was always going to be difficult but the initial 0-0 draw at Old Trafford is a great memory of mine personally. The Cup Winners Cup exit felt easier to take despite making it to the semi-final stage as we had won it the previous season.

Finishing in third place meant Chelsea had qualified for the Champions League for the next season for the first time in our history. It was a clear indication as to how far we had come and what a great job Gianluca Vialli was doing. Not searching for excuses but things could have been different if it wasn't for injuries to key players Gustavo Poyet, Tore Andre Flo and Pierluigi Casiraghi and of course losing Brian Laudrup.

Player of the year was deservedly Gianfranco Zola who also finished as the clubs top goal scorer with fifteen in all competitions. Goalkeeper Ed De Goey made the most first team appearances (forty-nine) and special mentions to Poyet and Flo with both being vital in a third place finish.

It was also a breakthrough season for Mikael Forssell and John Terry. All eyes were now on whether Chelsea could kick on and win the league whilst also competing in the Champions League.

1999 - 2000

Expectations going into the new season were most definitely high after coming close to winning the league. There was plenty of transfer activity as Chelsea would now be competing on Europe's biggest stage so squad depth was vital.

We said goodbye to Michael Duberry, Eddie Newton, Dmitri Kharine and Andy Myers. World Cup winning Captain Didier Deschamps joined from Juventus and so did striker Chris Sutton from Blackburn Rovers, a then club record fee of £10m. Other arrivals included Jess Hogh, Carlo Cudicini, Mario Melchiot, Gabriel Ambrosetti and later in the season Emerson Thome.

With Gianluca Vialli hanging up his boots it was time now for him to fully focus on managing the team.

Pre-season was low key for Chelsea with no involvement in tournaments etc with only a handful of individual games. Most notable was a testimonial for club captain Dennis Wise against Bologna, in front of a packed Stamford Bridge acknowledging ten years of service.

The excitement and anticipation for the new season was high and the arrival of striker Chris Sutton was huge after the unfortunate injury to Pierluigi Casiraghi. The real buzz though was the prospect of playing some of the best teams in Europe and making our debut in the Champions League.

Premier League
Date: Saturday 7th August 1999
Result: Chelsea 4-0 Sunderland
Chelsea Goal Scorers:
Poyet (20, 78), Zola (32), Flo (77)
Venue: Stamford Bridge

Attendance: 34,831

Chelsea Team:

De Goey, Ferrer, Desailly, Leboeuf, Petrescu (Di Matteo 86), Le Saux, Deschamps, Poyet (Babayaro 79), Wise, Sutton (Flo 73), Zola

The first game of the 1999/00 season saw newly promoted Sunderland visit Stamford Bridge. I remember me and my dad catching the earlier train to visit the Chelsea megastore. Since my birthday I was itching to get the new home shirt and this was the day I bought it. Caught up in the hype of the day I proceeded to have 'SUTTON 9' printed on the reverse and felt buzzing for the game. It was great to be back in our usual MHL seats and that first game is always nice to see familiar faces.

It took Chelsea twenty minutes to break the deadlock, a corner from Dennis Wise and Gustavo Poyet beating the goalkeeper to the ball to head home. It was soon 2-0 with Gianfranco Zola terrorising new signing and ex Arsenal defender Steve Bould before shooting across goal and finding the corner. It was most certainly a relief at half-time to be in control and it could have been more only for Sutton to fluff his lines on two occasions.

Tore Andre Flo replaced Sutton and scored within four minutes of being on the pitch. A lovely one two between Petrescu and Wise enabled Flo to head home from close range. Just a minute later it was 4-0 to The Blues and we all witnessed one the best goals Chelsea have ever scored and no doubt to be a contender for goal of the season, even on match day one! A fantastic twenty-yard pass over the top from new boy Didier Deschamps found Zola who cleverly flicked the ball over the defenders into the path of the arriving Poyet who volleyed into the top corner. A truly magical goal that rounded off the day perfectly. After the goal Chelsea fans sang to the travelling Sunderland fans, 'Welcome, to the Premiership. Welcome, to the Premiership'. To be fair they took it well with many of them chatting with us on the tube at Fulham Broadway and many clapping in appreciation for Poyet's winner. A great start to the new campaign.

It was back to Stamford Bridge just four days later for the first leg of our Champions League qualifier. Three late goals ensured a 3-0 victory against Skonto Riga with a second leg to come. Leicester away saw Chelsea snatch a point in injury time thanks to a last gasp own goal from former blue Frank Sinclair. Two 1-0 victories over Aston Villa and Wimbledon were either side of the second leg against Skonto Riga. A 0-0 draw was enough to see us through to the group stages. Chelsea would face Galatasaray, Hertha Berlin and a mouth-watering match up with European giants AC Milan.

Before we opened our European campaign against AC Milan we still had Newcastle to overcome. A 1-0 victory and another clean sheet in what was Bobby Robson's first game in charge after the sacking of Ruud Gullit.

The Champions League format would consist of two group stages before the quarter-finals. The top two in each group of four would qualify.

UEFA Champions League Group Stage, Match 1
Date: Wednesday 15th August 1999
Result: Chelsea 0-0 AC Milan
Venue: Stamford Bridge
Attendance: 33,873
Chelsea Team:
De Goey, Ferrer, Desailly, Leboeuf (Hogh 80), Petrescu, Babayaro, Deschamps, Poyet (Le Saux 79), Wise, Flo (Sutton 84), Zola

It's not often that fans remember 0-0 draws, however this one is referred to as one of the best many have ever seen at Stamford Bridge. The atmosphere on the night was electric and it really felt Chelsea had arrived in the big time playing one of the giants in European football. Not only was it amazing to see AC Milan at Stamford Bridge it was a game we really should have won.

Dennis Wise, Dan Petrescu and Tore Andre Flo all had chances in the first-half but couldn't convert. The second-half was also dominated by

Chelsea and despite Milan hitting the cross bar through Leonardo Chelsea came close as well. Zola hit the inside of the post with the ball rebounding into the goalkeepers arms and Petrescu had a well hit shot saved towards the end.

Of course we were close to victory but it was a performance to be very proud of with many neutrals praising Chelsea's efforts.

It was always going to be a test as to how we would cope in the league following exhausting European fixtures. That was apparent straight away with a disappointing 1-0 defeat at relegation tipped Watford. A 2-1 defeat to Hertha Berlin in Match Day Two made it look like an uphill task in the first group stage. Positive results soon followed with a 1-0 win at Middlesbrough and a memorable 1-0 victory over Galatasaray at Stamford Bridge. Going into the Manchester United game Chelsea had gained nine clean sheets in the first twelve games but even with the arrival of striker Chris Sutton we simply weren't scoring enough goals.

Premier League
Date: Sunday 3rd October 1999
Result: Chelsea 5-0 Manchester United
Chelsea Goal Scorers:
Poyet (1, 54), Sutton (16), Berg (o.g 59), Morris (81)
Venue: Stamford Bridge
Attendance: 34,909
Chelsea Team:
De Goey, Ferrer, Hogh, Leboeuf, Petrescu (Le Saux 77), Babayaro, Deschamps, Poyet, Wise (Morris 65), Zola (Flo 69), Sutton

Wow, wow, wow! Out of all the games mentioned in this book this is most definitely up there as one of the best. Fresh from winning the treble Chelsea faced Manchester United in a game many feared we'd get beaten.

Albert Ferrer crossed from the right hand side after just twenty-eight seconds with Gustavo Poyet beating the goalkeeper to the ball and heading into an empty net. What a great start, I wonder how many fans missed that one!

After fifteen minutes Chris Sutton made it 2-0 with a great header from a Dan Petrescu cross. Midway through the first-half things got even better as Nicky Butt was sent off for kicking Dennis Wise although Dennis seemed to provoke him.

Shortly after half-time Poyet scored his second of the match latching on to a rebound after an initial shot from Frank Leboeuf. Three quickly became four with Henning Berg scoring an own goal with Sutton lurking behind him. Stamford Bridge was absolutely rocking and substitute Jody Morris finished them off after another great move and celebrated famously with 'the trumpet'.

An important win and especially pleasing to score five goals. Chelsea were fantastic on the day and limited United to just one shot on goal all game. We were now three points off the top with two games in hand.

Despite expected changes to the line-up Chelsea suffered a shock home defeat to Huddersfield in the League Cup third round. A 1-0 defeat at Anfield followed and our dismal record there continued. Attentions then turned back to the Champions League.

UEFA Champions League Group Stage, Match 4
Date: Wednesday 20th October 1999
Result: Galatasaray 0-5 Chelsea
Chelsea Goal Scorers:
Flo (32, 49), Zola (54), Wise (79), Ambrosetti 87)
Venue: Ali Sami Yen Stadium, Istanbul
Attendance: 25,500
Chelsea Team:
De Goey, Ferrer, Desailly, Leboeuf, Babayaro, Le Saux, Deschamps (Wise 66), Morris, Poyet (Petrescu 66), Flo, Zola (Ambrosetti 75)

BLUE DAYS

Up until this point in the Champions League Chelsea had won, drawn and lost, this was a huge game. There was a lot of media attention around this fixture with Chelsea fans being warned about the dangers of travelling to the match. The Ali Sami Yen Stadium was nicknamed 'hell' and to say they would give Chelsea a hostile reception was an understatement.

Chelsea's players were greeted at the airport by Galatasaray fans doing everything they could to intimidate and bricks were thrown at the team bus. The players needed police protective shields covering them as they came onto the pitch to prevent missiles hitting them.

The Chelsea fans that made the trip proceeded to hang up a large flag in the away end reading, 'WELCOME TO HELL? WE'RE NOT BOTHERED'.

What happened next nobody could have predicted, another 5-0 thumping win and taking many by surprise. Two fantastic individual finishes either side of half-time from Tore Andre Flo put us in a great position. Ferrer's pass then put Zola through one-on-one with the goalkeeper where he finished with class. Substitute Dennis Wise made it 4-0 with an easy tap-in before Ambrosetti topped off a great night with a long-range effort. Chelsea inflicted the worst home defeat on Galatasaray and a shock win for Berlin over Milan put Chelsea in a very healthy position to qualify for the second group stage.

Before Chelsea went to Milan we lost 3-2 at home to Arsenal. The less said about that the better.

UEFA Champions League Group Stage, Match 5
Date: Tuesday 26th October 1999
Result: AC Milan 1-1 Chelsea
AC Milan Goal Scorer:
Bierhoff (74)
Chelsea Goal Scorer:
Wise (77)
Venue: San Siro, Milan

Attendance: 74,855

Chelsea Team:

De Goey, Ferrer, Desailly, Leboeuf, Petrescu (Morris 46), Babayaro, Deschamps, Poyet (Di Matteo 75), Wise, Flo, Zola (Ambrosetti 81)

No doubt this was going to be Chelsea's biggest test in the Champions League so far. After the performance against them at Stamford Bridge we could certainly go into the game believing we could get a positive result.

Chelsea had more than held their own and we were unfortunate to go 1-0 down fifteen minutes from time. Chelsea had come so close to taking the lead following a Poyet header that was saved from Wise's cross. Milan went straight up the other end and scored through Bierhoff.

I remember feeling gutted as we had played well and should have scored ourselves. Three minutes later, substitute Roberto Di Matteo made an instant impact and played a great ball through to Dennis Wise who slotted it clinically past the goalkeeper. A fantastic moment that led to the creation of a certain song about this goal which is still sung today.

The game finished 1-1 which was a very good result for us and a top performance to match. What always got me about this game was the number of Chelsea fans behind the goal, superb support. It was the highest attendance in a Chelsea match since the 1997 F.A Cup Final. A draw at home to Hertha Berlin would be enough for Chelsea to progress.

Our inconsistencies in the league were alarming and being part of a title race just didn't seem realistic if we were to progress in Europe. A poor 3-1 defeat at Derby reflected that which was then followed by a 2-0 victory over Hertha Berlin. Chelsea had now progressed to the second group stage where we would face Lazio, Feyenoord and Marseille.

A 0-0 draw at home to West Ham and a last gasp equaliser at Everton from Flo were on reflection disappointing results. Our European campaign was a completely different story with an impressive 3-1 win at home to Feyenoord. Our first league win in six came at home to Bradford City but was soon followed by an embarrassing 4-1 defeat at

Sunderland. The inconsistent results and performances were frustrating.

A 0-0 draw away to Lazio was a very important result and it was the return of the F.A Cup in December. A thumping 6-1 win at Hull with Poyet scoring a perfect hat-trick saw us progress to the fourth round. A 2-0 defeat at home to top of the league Leeds left Chelsea in tenth position.

Boxing Day saw The Blues travel to The Dell for the second year running. Much talk was of the Chelsea line-up as it was the first time an English club had fielded an entire eleven of foreign players. A load of media hype really on a day Chelsea won 2-1, a very much needed victory. Another three points at home to Sheffield Wednesday and draws against Coventry and Bradford led us to facing Tottenham at Stamford Bridge.

Premier League
Date: Wednesday 12th January 2000
Result: Chelsea 1-0 Tottenham Hotspur
Chelsea Goal Scorer:
Weah (87)
Venue: Stamford Bridge
Attendance: 34,969
Chelsea Team:
De Goey, Lambourde, Leboeuf, Terry, Thome, Harley, Petrescu, Di Matteo, Poyet (Sutton 56), Wise, Flo (Weah 56)

There was a lack of goals in this Chelsea team and it was quickly apparent that big money signing Chris Sutton wasn't working out and a new centre forward was needed. Former World Footballer of the Year George Weah signed for Chelsea on the day of the Spurs game on a loan deal until the end of the season. He had barely met his teammates but was registered in time to feature in the match.

It wasn't a particularly good game with Tottenham missing some good chances. However all that fans will remember was the introduction of George. Having literally just signed he got the winning goal three minutes from time heading in a Dennis Wise cross. An instant hero and our unbeaten record against Tottenham continued. I wasn't at this was one but my dad got to meet the man himself after the game. Waking up to a signed programme certainly softened the blow of not making the match.

A late Wise header at home to Leicester saw Chelsea now catch up with our games in hand and were now up to sixth in the league. A 2-0 victory over Nottingham Forest saw The Blues progress comfortably into the F.A Cup fifth round. A 0-0 draw at Aston Villa now saw Chelsea stretch to eight games without defeat but still not closing in on the European places.

As well as the positives in Europe we were also progressing in the F.A Cup, this time a 2-1 win over Leicester in the fifth round. The good results followed with wins over Spurs and Wimbledon before beating Gillingham 5-0 in the F.A Cup quarter-final and seeing a young John Terry score his first goal.

Beating Watford 2-1 saw The Blues undefeated in thirteen games, that was soon to change with a 1-0 defeat in Marseille, however what was pleasing was the reaction. A long trip to Newcastle soon after a European away had many thinking it wouldn't be our day. A 1-0 win thanks to Poyet put Chelsea up to third in the league. Chelsea would play Newcastle again in the F.A Cup semi-final at Wembley.

A 1-0 home win over Marseille thanks to Dennis Wise set us up nicely for the away trip to Feyenoord. A 1-1 draw at home to Everton happened shortly before that trip.

UEFA Champions League Group Stage 2, Match 5
Date: Tuesday 14th March 2000
Result: Feyenoord 1-3 Chelsea
Feyenoord Goal Scorer:
Kalou (59)

Chelsea Goal Scorers:
Zola (39), Wise (64), Flo (69)
Venue: De Kuip Stadium, Rotterdam
Attendance: 44,000
Chelsea Team:
De Goey, Desailly, Leboeuf, Petrescu, Babayaro, Deschamps, Di Matteo, Poyet (Morris 77), Wise, Flo, Zola (Ambrosetti 89)

Chelsea's Champions League campaign was fantastic and we were very much talked about by media outlets. A win against Feyenoord would see Chelsea progress to the quarter-final stage, quite unbelievable when thinking about how far the club had come.

Zola put us 1-0 up with a great shot on the turn from twenty-five yards, it was more than deserved as we had a number of chances before the breakthrough. In the second-half Feyenoord equalised through Salomon Kalou but five minutes later Chelsea restored the lead with a Babayaro cross finding Dennis Wise who headed in. The win was soon secured by a trademark Tore Andre Flo goal turning a defender inside out before curling the ball home.

We were now in the quarter-final with one game remaining, a great achievement.

A 0-0 draw away to West Ham saw Chelsea drop down to fifth position in a game we really should have won. A defeat at home to Lazio in the final group stage match saw us finish second. Chelsea would now face Barcelona over two legs, which was such an exciting prospect. Glenn Hoddle returned to Stamford Bridge with his Southampton side and earned a 1-1 draw. The next week was crucial for Chelsea with three huge games in three different competitions. A great 1-0 win at second-placed Leeds helped us to continue to fight for European places.

UEFA Champions League Quarter-final, First Leg
Date: Wednesday 5th April 2000
Result: Chelsea 3-1 Barcelona

Chelsea Goal Scorers:
Zola (30), Flo (34, 38)
Barcelona Goal Scorer:
Figo (64)
Venue: Stamford Bridge
Attendance: 33,662
Chelsea Team:
De Goey, Ferrer, Desailly, Thome, Petrescu (Di Matteo 71), Babayaro, Deschamps, Morris, Wise, Flo (Sutton 87), Zola

As soon as the Champions League quarter-final draw was made I made it very clear to my dad that I really wanted to go to this one, everyone wanted a ticket! It was such a huge occasion to see Chelsea play against Barcelona at Stamford Bridge. The nerves were flowing but I felt more excited about just being there. I actually think this was the only time I have ever purchased a half-and-half scarf, clearly a programme wasn't enough on this night as a memento.

In our usual MHL seats the atmosphere was electric. With the away fans still in the East Lower it always used to create a great atmosphere with the Matthew Harding Stand.

Chelsea were seriously pumped up for this one and Barcelona clearly didn't like it. On the half hour mark Luis Figo handled the ball just outside the box, it gave the referee no option other than to award Chelsea a free-kick. It was a Gianfranco Zola master class with him bending the ball over the wall and into the corner.

Four minutes after that Tore Andre Flo made it 2-0 with Zola now turning provider and Flo was able to tap-in from close range. The atmosphere and buzz around The Bridge was amazing but things soon got even better before half-time with Flo scoring his second of the match. It was Didier Deschamps who found Flo with a long ball and it was he who lobbed the goalkeeper from outside the box. Three goals in eight minutes, we were in dreamland.

We didn't stop singing throughout the game with fans making it clear where Barcelona could stick their Nou Camp! Unfortunately we couldn't stop them from scoring a vital away goal when Figo pulled one back with a clever finish.

The game finished 3-1 and a result we were very proud of, not many could have predicted that. The return leg in Barcelona would soon follow.

F.A Cup Semi-final
Date: Sunday 9th April 2000
Result: Newcastle 1-2 Chelsea
Newcastle Goal Scorer:
Lee (66)
Chelsea Goal Scorer:
Poyet (17, 72)
Venue: Wembley Stadium
Attendance: 73,876
Chelsea Team:
De Goey, Ferrer (Petrescu 74), Desailly, Leboeuf, Harley, Deschamps, Di Matteo, Poyet, Wise, Sutton (Flo 45), Weah

Another difficult game in prospect and another huge result, it wasn't our best performance by any stretch and it could be said that Newcastle may well have deserved it on the day.

A superb half volley lob from Gustavo Poyet put us in front but Newcastle deservedly equalised in the second-half.

Soon after Poyet met a fantastic Jon Harley cross to head home with Chelsea hanging on to victory. Despite another day at Wembley I look back on this game as one of those stressful ones. A game we were expected to win but it has to be said that Gustavo Poyet saved us that day.

The end of a huge week and three fantastic results, Chelsea would return to Wembley in the May to face Aston Villa in the F.A Cup Final.

A win at home to Coventry and a loss at Sheffield Wednesday

followed before the trip to Barcelona. The Champions League run finally came to an end at the Nou Camp but the 5-1 defeat doesn't tell the full story. Chelsea took the whole tie to extra-time thanks to an away goal by Tore Andre Flo. Chelsea were exhausted and gave absolutely everything and finished the game with ten men with Babayaro seeing red. We were proud of how far we went in the Champions League and had to except we were beaten by the best team in Europe.

Results in the league continued to be inconsistent but that was inevitable after going out of Europe and having the F.A Cup Final to focus on. Defeats at Highbury and Old Trafford followed with The Blues also drawing with Middlesbrough. We did however sign off in style at The Bridge beating Liverpool 2-0 and thumping Derby 4-0. It was also nice to see Mario Melchiot back to full fitness after missing most of the season through injury.

Chelsea finished in fifth place and needed to win the F.A Cup to avoid a summer Intertoto Cup appearance in order to qualify for Europe.

F.A Cup Final
Date: Saturday 20th May 2000
Result: Chelsea 1-0 Aston Villa
Chelsea Goal Scorer:
Di Matteo (73)
Venue: Wembley Stadium
Attendance: 78,217
Chelsea Team:
De Goey, Melchiot, Desailly, Leboeuf, Babayaro, Deschamps, Di Matteo, Poyet, Wise, Weah (Flo 88), Zola (Morris 89)

Another F.A Cup Final and one we could rest easy that we would get tickets without any issues. The build-up was still great but obviously didn't have the same feel as 1997. The players released the traditional F.A Cup Final song in the form of 'Blue Tomorrow' which was a thought for the title of this book.

We certainly went into the final as favourites but as we well know it's far from a certainty. It was quite a historic final being the first of the new millennium and the last to be played at the 'old Wembley' before it was knocked down and rebuilt. So that's what the history books will tell you, it certainly won't have a great deal of information about the game itself as it was pretty awful. However, when you win who cares?

Dennis Wise thought he had given Chelsea the lead but only to be judged offside, it was close! It was Roberto Di Matteo who scored the all important goal pouncing off a David James goalkeeping error in the second-half.

Great celebrations and relief when we scored and a real buzz seeing Dennis Wise lift yet another trophy. We decided after the game to get a mini bus back to Chelsea, fans celebrating down the Fulham Road with the pubs overflowing. The celebrations went on long into the night.

Another memorable day topped off with a victory bus parade through the streets of Fulham the next day.

Summary of the 1999/00 season

Finishing the Premier League season in fifth position and nowhere near challenging for the title certainly doesn't tell the story of this memorable season. To compete as well as we did in the club's first season in the Champions League and reaching the quarter-final stage was a great achievement as well as picking up more silverware in the form of the F.A Cup.

Chelsea played sixty-one competitive games which was the highest we'd ever played in one season.

There were certainly some fantastic games along the way which included the 5-0 win at home to Manchester United and away to Galatasaray. The Champions League nights were something special with Chelsea more than competing with the likes of Barcelona, AC Milan, Feyenoord and Lazio.

Dennis Wise was deservedly Chelsea's player of the year making fifty appearances. Goalkeeper Ed De Goey was top appearance maker taking to goal fifty-nine times. Tore Andre Flo finished as top goal scorer with nineteen in all competitions with Gustavo Poyet close behind. A special mention also has to go to George Weah, making an instant impact following his loan in January.

2000 - 2001

It was another eventful summer at Stamford Bridge with chairman Ken Bates more than happy to give Gianluca Vialli funds to strengthen the squad. Chelsea made a £4m loss on Chris Sutton by selling him to Celtic but in came Jimmy Floyd Hasselbaink for £15m from Atletico Madrid.

Young Icelandic striker Eidur Gudjohnsen joined for £4m from Bolton Wanderers, Mario Stanic, Winston Bogarde and Christian Panucci (loan) also joined the squad. Didier Deschamps joined Valencia for £2.3m and we said farewell to Tore Andre Flo who later in the season joined Rangers for £12m.

Expectations at Chelsea were once again high especially with the signing of Hasselbaink. Chelsea had been desperately unlucky with centre forwards with the injury to Casiraghi and the disappointment of Sutton.

Chelsea would participate in the UEFA Cup but with already having a taste of the Champions League this was thought by many as being more of a distraction.

Nothing of real significance happened in pre-season due to Euro 2000 until we faced Manchester United in the Charity Shield at Wembley.

F.A Charity Shield
Date: Sunday 13th August 2000
Result: Chelsea 2-0 Manchester United
Chelsea Goal Scorers:
Hasselbaink (22), Melchiot (72)
Venue: Wembley Stadium
Attendance: 65,148

Chelsea Team:
De Goey, Melchiot, Desailly, Leboeuf, Babayaro, Di Matteo (Morris 70), Poyet (Le Saux 76), Stanic, Wise, Hasselbaink, Zola (Gudjohnsen 72)

With the anticipation of the new season Chelsea's Wembley allocation was a sell out. Although I appreciate the Charity Shield is classed as a friendly it certainly wasn't played like it on the pitch and Blues fans seemed particularly up for this one. There was a group of ten of us and with my brother now finished University he bought his own season ticket with his friend (more games for me).

Now being seventeen I was more inclined to have a few beers with my dad on a match day and this was most certainly the case on this day. We started early and all met up at the Stage Door pub at Victoria for beers and food. There was certainly a good vibe going into this one with confidence for the new season high. Winning the F.A Cup the previous season was great but Manchester United fans often reminded us that they did not participate in it as they played in the FIFA Club World Cup. That certainly added extra spice to this one and the fact it was the last time we'd be visiting Wembley before it was knocked down and rebuilt.

The atmosphere on the tube to Wembley Park was great with Chelsea fans in full voice and this continued when walking down Wembley way. Once we were in the stadium it did have a cup final feel and with limited hospitality in those days it really was a 'sea of blue'.

Chelsea took the lead on twenty-two minutes and it was new signing Jimmy Floyd Hasselbaink that got his Chelsea career off to the perfect start with a deflected shot from close range. It was more than deserved with The Blues dominating from the first whistle.

With Chelsea still very much in control Roy Keane was sent off on the hour after a poor challenge on Poyet. From what I can remember he was lucky to be on the pitch for that long. Ten minutes after that Mario Melchiot secured the win with a clever run before placing the ball into the bottom corner from outside the box. A great moment in front of the Chelsea fans and pleased for him having spent much of his Chelsea career out with injury.

A good day at Wembley with drinks flowing throughout. We headed back to Chelsea after and had a few drinks in the Shed Bar. Smiles all round topped off perfectly with Ken Bates going out of his way to give Sir Alex Ferguson his loser's medal.

Premier League
Date: Saturday 19th August 2000
Result: Chelsea 4-2 West Ham United
Chelsea Goal Scorers:
Hasselbaink (31 pen), Zola (59), Stanic (78, 90)
West Ham Goal Scorers:
Di Canio (48), Kanoute (85)
Venue: Stamford Bridge
Attendance: 34,914
Chelsea Team:
De Goey, Melchiot, Panucci, Desailly, Babayaro (Le Saux 69), Di Matteo, Poyet (Morris 81), Stanic, Wise, Hasselbaink, Zola (Flo 69)

The season properly kicked off with a London derby against West Ham at Stamford Bridge. I'd been in the pubs around Chelsea many times in the past but now it felt very different, the beers were flowing! From Brogans to the Britannia we were most certainly up for this one.

Jimmy Floyd Hasselbaink carried on his fine form from the Charity Shield by converting a penalty that he won after half an hour. Di Canio equalised shortly after half-time with a very clever finish. Gianfranco Zola restored our lead on the hour with a trademark free-kick from twenty-five yards.

The moment of the match happened soon after with another debutant Mario Stanic, ball juggling before unleashing a shot on the volley from thirty-five yards. His shot was quite unbelievable which landed in the top corner, I was sat right behind it, one of the best.

West Ham made it 3-2 from a corner with Kanoute scoring a header after some poor Chelsea defending. However, it didn't matter as Stanic wrapped up the win as we approached the ninety minutes heading in a cross from Roberto Di Matteo. A great win and confidence was certainly high, further drinks followed at the Slug and Lettuce. Snakebite £2, Apple Sours £1. It was a good day.

CONCLUSION

Confidence was high after beating both Manchester United and West Ham but things didn't continue positively. A dreadful 2-0 defeat at relegation favourites Bradford was followed by three draws against Aston Villa, Arsenal and Newcastle. That was enough to see Gianluca Vialli sacked on September 12th.

Again it was a shock as the fans still had confidence in Vialli. Despite a great run in the Champions League and an F.A Cup success it could have been seen from the board that we were falling further away from a title challenge after investing much money into the team.

Claudio Ranieri eventually took over with Chelsea finishing in sixth position. I also look back fondly on Claudio's time at Chelsea and despite being known as 'the tinkerman' he continues to be well thought of. He was most certainly part of a transitional period before Roman Abramovich bought the club. It shouldn't be forgotten that he signed Frank Lampard for £11 million from West Ham in the summer of 2001 and took the club to an F.A Cup Final in 2002. Securing Champions League qualification in 2003 was huge with the club in much financial difficulty. Under Claudio Chelsea also finished second in the Premier League in 2003/04 and reached the Champions League semi-final.

As we well know the appointment of Jose Mourinho soon followed with Chelsea then going on to the next level by winning the club's first League title for fifty years in 2005.

Roman's arrival in 2003 has taken the club to another level and what we have achieved can only be described as magical. Many rivals thought that Chelsea were lucky to have Roman's investment and why didn't he choose another other club.

The answer for me is simple, Chelsea were a sleeping giant, not only that but the foundations were already there and it all started with

Glenn Hoddle, Ruud Gullit and Gianluca Vialli.

GATE 17
THE COMPLETE COLLECTION
(NEW YEAR 2021)

CHELSEA
Over Land and Sea – Mark Worrall
Chelsea here, Chelsea There – Kelvin Barker, David Johnstone, Mark Worrall
Chelsea Football Fanzine – the best of cfcuk
One Man Went to Mow – Mark Worrall
Chelsea Chronicles (Five Volume Series) – Mark Worrall
Making History Not Reliving It –
Kelvin Barker, David Johnstone, Mark Worrall
Celery! Representing Chelsea in the 1980s – Kelvin Barker
Stuck On You: a year in the life of a Chelsea supporter – Walter Otton
Palpable Discord: a year of drama and dissent at Chelsea – Clayton Beerman
Rhyme and Treason – Carol Ann Wood
Eddie Mac Eddie Mac – Eddie McCreadie's Blue & White Army
The Italian Job: A Chelsea thriller starring Antonio Conte – Mark Worrall
Carefree! Chelsea Chants & Terrace Culture – Mark Worrall, Walter Otton
Diamonds, Dynamos and Devils – Tim Rolls
Arrivederci Antonio: The Italian Job (part two) – Mark Worrall
Where Were You When We Were Shocking? – Neil L. Smith
Chelsea: 100 Memorable Games – Chelsea Chadder
Bewitched, Bothered & Bewildered – Carol Ann Wood
Stamford Bridge Is Falling Down – Tim Rolls
Cult Fiction – Dean Mears
Chelsea: If Twitter Was Around When… – Chelsea Chadder
Blue Army – Vince Cooper
Liquidator 1969-70 A Chelsea Memoir – Mark Worrall
When Skies Are Grey: Super Frank, Chelsea And The Coronavirus Crisis – Mark Worrall
Tales Of The (Chelsea) Unexpected – David Johnstone & Neil L Smith
The Ultimate Unofficial Chelsea Quiz Book – Chelsea Chadder
Let The Celery Decide – Walter Otton
Blue Days – Chris Wright

FICTION
Blue Murder: Chelsea Till I Die – Mark Worrall
The Wrong Outfit – Al Gregg
The Red Hand Gang – Walter Otton
Coming Clean – Christopher Morgan
This Damnation – Mark Worrall
Poppy – Walter Otton

NON FICTION
Roe2Ro – Walter Otton
Shorts – Walter Otton
England International Football Team Quiz & Trivia Book – George Cross

www.gate17.co.uk

Printed in Great Britain
by Amazon